The On Deck Circle of Life

The On Deck Circle of Life

101 Lessons from the Dugout

Harley A. Rotbart, M.D.

iUniverse, Inc.
New York Lincoln Shanghai

The On Deck Circle of Life
101 Lessons from the Dugout

Copyright © 2007 by Harley A. Rotbart

iUniverse books may be ordered through booksellers or by contacting:

iUniverse
2021 Pine Lake Road, Suite 100
Lincoln, NE 68512
www.iuniverse.com
1-800-Authors (1-800-288-4677)

The views expressed in this work are solely those of the author and do not necessarily reflect the views of the publisher, and the publisher hereby disclaims any responsibility for them.

Cover design by Tommy Kubitsky, © 2007.

ISBN-13: 978-0-595-42390-3 (pbk)
ISBN-13: 978-0-595-86726-4 (ebk)
ISBN-10: 0-595-42390-6 (pbk)
ISBN-10: 0-595-86726-X (ebk)

Printed in the United States of America

To Mickey Owen, who allowed the infamous passed ball in the 1941 World Series that propelled the New York Yankees to beat his Brooklyn Dodgers.

And to Bill Buckner, who let the fateful ground ball get through his legs at 1st base in the 1986 World Series, helping the New York Mets beat his Boston Red Sox.

The pain caused by those errors was long ago overshadowed by the life lessons we learned from them.

Baseball is like church. Many attend, few understand.

Leo Durocher (1906-1991), Hall of Fame baseball manager

ACKNOWLEDGEMENTS

Much love and many thanks to:

Sara, who shares the bleachers and blankets with me, keeps the scorebook, brings the refreshments, washes the uniforms, and teaches our kids how to have fun.

Matt, Emily, and Sam for being the 3 most wonderful reasons to coach.

My mom, who took us to Denver Bears baseball games and waited with us outside the locker room to collect autographs; and my dad, who had to imagine what a real baseball field looked like while listening to Bears games on the radio in his truck at work.

Ruth, Gene, Donald, Barbara, Dean, Talya, Maxwell, Avital, Laurie, Bill, Carolyn, Becky, Joanie, Ron and Bernd for being my fans.

Bart Schmitt, Paul Offit, and Kevin Kalikow for being my role models as doctor-writers.

Mark Barter, Matty Feldman, Jeff Fisher, Jack Makovsky, Ken Mason, Jim Nogami, and Mike Wolfe, for being my role models as coaches.

CONTENTS

The On Deck Circle of Life

ON BASE

The On Deck Circle of Life

ON THE MOUND

EXTRA INNINGS

INTRODUCTION FOR PARENTS

Congratulations! You and your kids are fans of the greatest games on earth! You may not realize it yet, but as baseball and softball fans you have acquired unique insight into the secrets for a happy and successful life. Either because your kids are among the nearly 20 million in the U.S. who play the games, or because you watch the pros play, you have learned hidden truths from the oracle of baseball. But, they are *well*-hidden truths, and you may not even have noticed your enlightenment. That's why you and your kids need to read this book.

THE ON DECK CIRCLE OF LIFE is written in a style, and at a level, that both you and your kids can enjoy, separately or together. Like everything else where kids are concerned, it's more fun together. Kids will find familiar baseball scenarios, followed by comparable real-life situations that they have already experienced or will experience as they grow. Adults will find invaluable tools for child-raising, lessons that every parent should teach their children about life.

ON DECK is organized into 101 vignettes, or "chapters", divided among 6 sections—*In the dugout, At the plate, On base, In the field, On the mound,* and *Extra innings.* The chapters can be read in any sequence and in any combination, whenever the moment is right. The format of each chapter is simple—individual facets of the game are presented in an easy to understand, concise, parable-like style. These are all very familiar to you and your kids. The lineup card, the batting order, keeping score, home field advantage, the strikeout, the walk, the sacrifice, the pickle, hit and run, stealing, sliding, the double play, the grounder, home runs, around-the-horn, errors, the umpire, averages, heroes and goats. Following each baseball metaphor is a pearl of wisdom or two from the dugout, the real-world messages and meanings that your kids need to learn. Lessons about self-esteem, honesty, courage, friendship, gratitude, persistence, altruism, stigmas, patience, stereotypes and prejudice. Advice on overcoming fears, coping with pain, adapting to change, planning ahead, believing in yourself, respecting others, defining success, developing good habits, learning from mistakes, and making the most of every opportunity.

101 fundamental principles for future happiness and success in the major leagues of school, friendships, and family life.

You may think that you and your kids know baseball. And you do—at least the rules and the strategy. But, like reading encrypted text, many of the underlying lessons that baseball has to offer are subliminal, too subtle to easily appreciate. By decoding those secret missives, *ON DECK* becomes an indispensable communication tool for you as parents, putting you on common ground—or a common base path, to stay in the motif—with your kids. Your kids already understand how to "wait for the right pitch", "take a bigger leadoff", "tag up", "lay one down", and "call it". Yet, they stare blankly as you lecture them to use good judgment and common sense, balance risks with rewards, control angry and impulsive behavior, give of themselves for others, and take responsibility for their actions. *ON DECK* teaches kids of all ages that picking the right pitch to swing at is the ultimate exercising of good judgment and common sense; that a runner leading off base perfectly demonstrates the balance of risk and reward; that the self-discipline of tagging up rather than running with the crack of the bat is true impulse control; that bunting shows the value of sacrificing for others; and, that calling for the pop fly asserts leadership and accepts responsibility. *ON DECK* teaches your kids how to deal with the real world challenges that face them, using the baseball vignettes and vernacular that they already understand. It is a book of baseball wisdom for life, drawn from the everyday, every play circumstances of the diamond. And, I predict, you will find that *ON DECK's* lessons are as relevant for adulthood as for childhood.

Okay, you ask, who is this guy and what's he doing writing a book about baseball? My troubles started when I began coaching my own kids' teams in 1993. With 1, 3, and 5 year olds at home, my wife and I were consumed by the overwhelming young neurotic parent syndrome of wanting to be the perfect teachers, role models, and inspirations to our children. In my case, the neurosis was worsened by all my years as a pediatrician—I, of all people, should know how to raise perfect children! This preoccupation with parenting perfection inevitably extended onto the playing fields where I coached. I wanted to teach my players more than baseball—I wanted them to learn about everything important in their lives. I found myself using baseball metaphors to guide my players and my own kids through their real world issues—and they seemed to get it. It wasn't long before I was using baseball parables to help my patients and their parents through their developmental years together, and even through the maze of medical care. Ultimately, I came to the epiphany that everything that occurs on the baseball field is a microcosmic reflection of the real world.

My wife Sara shares the bleachers with me and has long encouraged me to write down all of my whispered profundities. Although I've suspected she really just wanted me to keep quiet and let her watch the games, I began taking her advice and writing. Our kids, Matt, Emily, and Sam, think I'm too picky when I help them proofread their schoolwork, but they tolerate me in the dugout. Our dog Lizzy doesn't really have any major complaints that I've heard about, and she particularly appreciates how coaching has improved my fetch throwing.

So that's how I came to write a book about baseball. Although, as you'll see, it isn't really about baseball at all.

INTRODUCTION FOR KIDS

Yes, it's true, baseball and softball are the greatest games on earth. But did you know that I've convinced your parents that *reading* about baseball and softball is good for you? That's one reason they bought this book. So, read it!

The chapters are really short. The top half of each chapter is about baseball, and the bottom half is about the rest of your life. See if you can figure out how they are connected. If you can, your parents will think you're really smart. If you can't, ask your parents and that will make them feel really smart. That's the other reason they bought this book.

The title of the book is *THE ON DECK CIRCLE OF LIFE*. See the connection? Being a kid is like standing in the on deck circle for becoming a grown-up. What you learn as a kid *on deck* will help you when you're up to bat as an adult in the real world. In the *Introduction* I wrote for your parents, I didn't tell them what the book title really means, so please explain it to them in case they don't get it.

Hope you enjoy the book. **Play ball!**

IN THE DUGOUT

 **CHAPTER 1**

KEEPING SCORE

Legendary players, legendary games, legendary moments. Baseball's moments are officially recorded in the scorebook, where each event on the field has its own special symbol or code. At the end of each game and at the end of each season, the accomplishments and performances of each player can be counted, averaged, summarized and analyzed. The exact number and types of hits and outs. How many pitches a pitcher threw, and how many for strikes. Whether the ground ball out was hit to the 3rd baseman or to the shortstop. Much more important, though, is what's *not* recorded in the scorebook—the spirit and soul of the at-bat, the guts and gumption of the pitcher, the hustle and heroics of the fielders. Legendary performances are recorded in the hearts and minds of the players, coaches, and fans. A caught fly ball is scored the same way in the book, whether it was a routine pop-up or a running, diving, acrobatic catch at the fence. But brilliant plays and dazzling efforts are scored and stored in the memories of everyone at the game long after the numbers and statistics are crunched and the scorebook is closed.

From the dugout

You are much more than just a list of your accomplishments. It's not only *what* you do, but *how* you do it that counts in the real scorebook of your life. Making the spectacular diving catch says more about you than the "out" that is recorded in the scorebook. It says you have game. It says you give 110%. Every performance in your life becomes a choice you have to make. Will you do just enough to get by, letting the ball drop in front of you for a base hit? Or will you push yourself to perform like an all-star, the legendary player you know you can be, and dive for the ball? Your special effort will be recorded in the minds and memories of others. More importantly you will have the peace of mind and self-respect that come from knowing that you gave your very best—even if you don't end up making the catch. That's the stuff of legends.

 **CHAPTER 2**

THE STARTING LINEUP

As the fans are settling into their seats before every game, a growing suspense is *unsettling* the players in the dugout who wait and worry about their assignments. Who's starting and who's not? There's only room for nine players to start each game; on most teams, an almost equal number are left sitting on the bench when the game begins.

From the dugout

Every player can't start each game. Life has more players for most opportunities than there are starting roles. Not everyone can be "first chairs" in the orchestra, leads in the school play, soloists in the choir, winners of the election, committee chairs, or class representatives. If you're named a starter in any of life's games, don't assume that you'll always be a starter; keep earning your spot with each play and even between plays. Hustle; improve your skills; be a role model for others; be gracious and never gloat. Remember that you're part of a team. On the other hand, when life doesn't put you in the starting line-up, work hard and try to be a starter for the next game. Even if you end up on the bench more than you play, you can make important contributions—cheer for your teammates, follow the game, keep the scorebook, help with the equipment. Your day will come, even if it's not in this game or in this season. Prove to your coach, and to yourself, that you're ready to come into the game when called.

More from the dugout

Don't judge yourself through the eyes of others. The coach has his own reasons for his starting picks, but coaches are human and make mistakes, too. Because this coach or the next doesn't consider you a starter, you should always see yourself as a starter.

The On Deck Circle of Life

Others' opinions of your abilities and potential may be way off—only *you* know yourself well enough to judge *you*. Rejections are part of everyone's life—they will come from coaches, teachers, college admissions offices, boyfriends, girlfriends, bosses. The only rejection you should *never* experience is from yourself. Whatever others think of you, know yourself. You are a starter, whether you find yourself on the field or on the bench for this particular game.

CHAPTER 3

PLAYING TIME

A mysterious formula explains how much time the coach lets each player play. The equation involves some combination of: Ability, Age, Attendance and Attitude; add Academics for school teams. What varies from coach to coach is how much value they put on each of the A's. Some coaches go with ability—the best players play the most. Other coaches reward positive attitude and perfect attendance more than they do pure baseball skills. Some coaches give the older kids more time because the younger kids will be back next season when they'll be the older kids.

From the dugout

There is more than one way to earn your spot and increase your playing time on any team. What qualifies you to play in life's games is a combination of your actual skills, and harder to measure factors like a positive attitude, hard work, and team spirit. Your energy, enthusiasm, and commitment affect the decisions people make about you; if you pout and sulk, your chances of playing will be worse, and when you do play, you'll enjoy it less.

More from the dugout

Unfortunately, how much you get to play may be a pretty random decision. Better players may spend more time on the bench than less talented ones. The hardest workers and most enthusiastic teammates may not even get noticed. In life, there isn't always a good formula to explain why good people are sometimes treated badly. Try your hardest and be the best you can be. In most cases, it will pay off—you'll play more and be more successful. But sometimes, stuff happens, and fairness may be fantasy. Take comfort knowing that you've done everything you can and that the outcome wasn't your fault. Move on and hope that fate plays more fairly the next time.

Still more from the dugout

It's okay to challenge your playing time if you do it politely and respectfully. "Coach, it's not fair! I'm as good as Johnny and work twice as hard but he gets to play more than me" isn't polite or respectful. "Coach, what do I need to do to get in the game more—I'll try harder, come earlier to practice for extra batting or fielding work, whatever it takes" is both polite *and* respectful. It also has several important effects on the coach. It reminds him that you're not playing a lot (remember, coaches are human—he may have lost track of your time on the field), it reminds him of your positive attitude, and it makes him feel a little guilty (not a bad thing). When you gently challenge the decisions of the important people in your life, it may help them appreciate you more—the thoughtful coach is now more conscious of you and your role on the team, and more careful about being fair. The same is true with your teachers, your bosses, and, yes, even your parents (being polite and respectful is especially important when you challenge your parents' decisions!). If you ask what more you can do and you learn you've actually already been doing it, your coach or teacher (even your parents) will be more aware of your achievements. On the other hand—you may be shocked to learn that there *really are* skills that you haven't mastered yet and should be working on. You now have a better idea about how the decisions were made, and you have a new plan for increasing your playing time.

CHAPTER 4

BATTING ORDER

There's a lot of folklore, and some foolishness, involved in the batting order. The image of the leadoff hitter is much different from the clean-up hitter (4th to hit), and both are completely different from the image of the batter hitting 9th. Coaches talk about "classic number 2 and number 3 hitters". Speed, strength, consistency, hand-eye coordination, and other hard to measure factors all go into the coach's decision about who bats when. Really, though, it only matters for the first inning, until the first 3 outs are made by the hitting team. After that, any batter might lead off an inning; any batter might come up with runners in scoring position. Hits are just as important for number 9 batters as they are for leadoff hitters. But batting order labels affect how players feel about themselves, and often how they perform. Batters in the number 3 and 4 spots think of themselves as the best hitters while batters hitting 8 and 9 think of themselves as the worst. The number 7 batter feels less important to the team than the number 2 batter.

From the dugout

You're only a number 9 hitter if you believe the label and start to think like one. As you play through the innings of your life, you determine your own success at the plate, regardless of how you are labeled by others. In everything you do, you will be characterized, categorized, and classified. "Fast group" in reading, "slow group" in math, "gifted and talented", "learning challenged", "honor roll", "troublemaker", "born leader", "follows the crowd". If someone brands you a number 9 hitter in any part of your life, don't fall for it. If you start to believe the labels that others give you, you may also start to hit the way you think that label should hit and act the way you think that label should act. Ignore the labels. Play every game the best you can, no matter what the expectations are of those around you.

More From the Dugout

Positive labels can have negative effects, too. A good hitter who's been batting 8th may suddenly slump when he's named the new leadoff or clean-up hitter. Expectations come with the title, and the pressure of those expectations can be great. Whatever someone else calls you, you are still you. Your coach, your teacher, or your boss may believe that by rewarding you with a new position, you will magically acquire new abilities to fill that role. You may start to believe that, too. The combined weight of others' expectations and your own may make you slump and fail. A new title or label means that your performance *up until now* has been noticed and appreciated, and that you have promise for even better in the future. It does not mean that you will immediately become that new title. Give yourself time to grow into a new role. Expect a lot from yourself, but be reasonable—the Hall of Fame isn't earned in a day. The skills that made you successful enough to earn your new label will continue to carry you as you develop into your new spot in the batting order.

CHAPTER 5

THE UNIFORM

Game day has a special elegance because baseball has a strict dress code. At practices, players look shabby, shaggy, and disconnected. But on game day, teams wear crisp, matching uniforms, coordinated down to their socks and belts. Hats are all turned brim-forward. Cleats are good, sneakers are bad. The "coolest" kids dress just like the others. Umpires strictly enforce the rules: helmets on the hitting team; jerseys tucked into pants; watches, jewelry, and other distractions stay in the dugout. Game day's wardrobe is designed to be both tasteful and safe. The uniform also raises the performance of the team, bringing greater sense of harmony and importance to what they do.

From the dugout

There is a time to be an individual and a time to blend in. Calling attention to yourself during a team effort takes away from your teammates and from your team. Someone always shows up for their school assembly with spiked purple hair, or attends his high school graduation wearing nothing but boxers under his gown, and attracts the attention and giggles that he was looking for. The shortest skirt or lowest cut blouse in the classroom always gets the stares and whistles. But when everyone is looking at you, your team loses its importance and its dignity. When you show off, you are really showing that you are insecure about who you are. Stand out by your play, your hustle, and your positive attitude, not by your inappropriate behavior or outlandish clothes in the wrong places at the wrong times. When the game's over, tear off your uniform and cleats and become the individual you are, in T-shirts, shorts and sandals—or whatever separates you from the crowd. But during the game, at school, and at work, wear the uniform that fits the setting, and blend in for the good of the team.

CHAPTER 6

EQUIPMENT

Since the discovery of fire and the invention of the wheel, we have known that the right tools improve both the product and the performance. Baseball's tools are highly specialized. Different fielding gloves are designed for catchers, first basemen, infielders, and outfielders. Bats are made with nearly precious metals, each more rare and mysterious sounding than the other. Every year brings more expensive and more complicated equipment. The latest bat is guaranteed to give added "pop", the newest glove designed for a "truer pocket" and "easier snap". When a teammate shows up with this year's hot and expensive new item, the dugout buzzes. Every player needs to hold it, try it out.

From the dugout

Why should baseball gear be different than equipment for the rest of life, where each new and more expensive toy adds higher definition, greater fidelity, faster acceleration, more pixels? But, when you judge value by how much something costs, you can forget what's really valuable. How much "pop" does a bat need to hit the ball well? Watch what happens when all your teammates try out the new plutonium weapon. Yes, the strong hitters may hit the ball a little farther with the super-bats, but those hitters led the team with their old bats, too. The medium hitters continue to hit medium—maybe the ball comes off the bat a little harder, maybe not. The outcome of their season doesn't change, and average players don't become superstars by changing equipment. A great photographer will take great pictures with a great camera; she will also take great pictures with a good camera. A concert pianist will sound fabulous on a Steinway Grand, but will sound almost as fabulous on the well-tuned upright. As a hitter, you get better by practice, training, and conditioning. Your swing, not what you are swinging, determines how hard and how far the ball is hit. The next time a new piece of equipment shows up in your dugout, remember that this year's hot new thing will be next year's old news. But the basic values and skills you develop will last from year to year. And if you save enough money on the bats you use, someday you'll be able to afford a good camera and piano, too.

More from the dugout

Expensive equipment raises expectations and distracts from the accomplishment. When you step to the plate with the hot new stick in your hands, the weak ground ball you hit seems all the more disappointing—to you, to your teammates, and to your parents who paid for the bat! And when you hit a home run using a super-bat, the bat steals some of the credit in the minds of those watching, and in your own mind. On the other hand, when you perform brilliantly with standard equipment, all the credit goes to you, with no one thinking "it's the bat".

Still more from the dugout

More may be less. Sometimes, new and fancy equipment can even make your performance *worse*. The weight and balance of a new bat may not be as comfortable for you as your old bat. The specialized first baseman's glove, with it's extra-long shape, extra webbing, and deeper pocket, may cause fielding and catching errors that you never would have made with your familiar old fielder's glove. Different isn't always good; new isn't always better, and expensive isn't always best.

CHAPTER 7

PINCH HITTERS AND PINCH RUNNERS

During the game, eager and anxious substitute players wait on the dugout bench to get in and play. Substitutions in the middle of a game are common. They let coaches put in a good hitter or fast runner at an important moment, and let players who haven't played yet get into the game before it ends. A player who hits better than he fields can be a big help off the bench as a pinch hitter. The player who doesn't hit *or* field well can usually run—and a good pinch runner can also make an important contribution to a team.

From the dugout

Even though you would rather play than sit while others play, you should still feel badly when a teammate doesn't get into the game. When your friend doesn't have a chance to participate, it changes the feeling on the team. A loss is harder to take, and a win is less exciting if everyone doesn't feel that they are a part of the effort. Imagine yourself as the one who doesn't get to play. How will you feel at the end of the game? Life is full of chances to exclude people. From clubs, cliques, and carpools to sororities, societies and study groups, there are always those who others would keep out. When it's up to you, include, don't exclude. You'll feel better, the others will feel better, and the group will be a better group. It may be tempting to follow the the "cool crowd" who find you worthy, but enjoy keeping others out. Don't join them. Speak up for the outsiders—and consider whether you really want to be part of a group that acts that way to your other friends. The same group may change its mind about you someday. Every game can use a pinch runner or a pinch hitter, and every pinch player becomes part of the team effort, making the group stronger and raising the spirit in the dugout.

 **CHAPTER 8**

ON DECK

The greatest opportunity during a game for instant learning and preparation is when a batter is "on deck". When a player is the next up to bat, he is allowed out of the dugout and onto the field to stand in a specially marked spot, the "on deck circle", with an up-close view of the pitcher and the action at home plate. Being on deck gives the next batter an important preview of what the immediate future holds for him. The pitcher's motion, emotion, and habits, as well as the variety and speed of his pitches, are all on display for the player paying close attention in the on deck circle. He also gets a good look at the umpire and the boundaries of his strike zone.

From the dugout

Prepare in advance. When you're on deck, pretend that you're the batter. Focus on every pitch. Stand like the batter, swing with each pitch, time your swing to the pitcher's delivery. Sometimes life gives you a preview of the challenges about to come your way. Be observant—this is your crystal ball, a chance to know the unknown. Whenever you're allowed on deck—on the baseball field, in school, at home, or at work—with a chance to learn from those ahead of you, use it as a heads-up and a head start. If you're asleep or fooling around in the on deck circle, you've missed a golden opportunity to improve your upcoming performance.

More from the dugout

The reason the "on deck circle" is so close to the batter is because the view is better there than anywhere else on the field. A better view means a clearer focus on the details of what's going on. Sit in the front of the classroom at school. Your classmates in the back row, like those squirting water at each other in the dugout, are missing the finer points, and distracting each other from where the attention of the class should be focused. The results from the back row are never as good as those that come from sitting up close.

AT THE PLATE

CHAPTER 9

THE BATTER'S BOX

The chalk lines around a baseball diamond come together at the small space surrounding home plate where the batter stands to face the pitcher. When the batter is "in the box", the pitcher can throw the ball; when the batter steps out of the box, the pitcher waits. The batter forms a plan each time he steps into the box. For slow pitchers, he stands "up in the box", as close to the front as possible; if the pitcher is fast, the batter plants himself "back in the box", furthest away, to allow the most time to react to the pitch. Some hitters "crowd", inching as close to the plate as they can, giving them better reach for the outside corner; others stand further away, either by habit or because they're afraid of being hit. It's inside this few square inches of dirt that the batter tries to put himself in the best position to face the pitcher for the man-on-man battle that only one of the two will win.

From the dugout

When you step into the batter's box, you are the only person in the game with the right and the requirement to be in that position at that moment. Even if there are 8 other players who are stronger or more confident hitters, it's now up to you. Even when the pitcher is frightening and the coach is coaxing and the fans are praying, you're the man. You must now "step up to the plate". There are many situations in life where you, and you alone, will have to take a stand, assume responsibility—ready or not. Be ready. And be willing and eager and self-confident. Preparing in advance and taking lots of practice are valuable tools for being *ready*. But *willing* and *eager* and *self-confident* come from deep inside you. Before you're up, be the batter who can't wait to step into the batter's box. During your at bat, stare down and boldly battle the pitcher. And, the moment this at-bat is finished, start looking forward to your next one. You are the right player for this moment. Even if you fail this time, you'll be the right player for your next at-bat. If you weren't the right player, you wouldn't have come out for the team, wouldn't have made the team, wouldn't have been put in the lineup, and wouldn't now be standing in the box. The situations in life that call for you to step up to the plate are calling *you* because *you* are the right person for the job. Believe in yourself and in your ability to face any challenge the game has to offer. You are in the batter's box where you belong.

More from the dugout

The differences between "up in the box", "back in the box", "crowding" and standing further from the plate are only a matter of inches—it's a very small box, after all. But the effect of moving an inch or two in one direction or the other can be great—if not on your actual physical ability to hit the pitch, at least in your comfort as a batter—which may in turn help you hit the pitch. Small moves in life's other batter's boxes can also make a difference in your actual ability or comfort level, or both. The best way to get comfortable in life's batter's boxes is to get into them early. Rushing in at the last minute before class, a test, a performance, an airplane trip, a doctor's appointment, a meeting, or other important events doesn't let you find your comfort zone in the box. It throws you off your game plan and makes it harder to find the best position to get a hit. But, when you arrive early you have enough time to pick a good seat, sharpen your pencil, find a rest room, arrange your desk, hang up your coat and, finally, comfortably settle in for the pitch.

CHAPTER 10

HEY BATTER, BATTER

Baseball games are noisy places. Fans are cheering, coaches are yelling, and players are shouting advice to their teammates. There's often another kind of noise as well. There are still teams that chatter, taunting the opposing team's batter, or pitcher, or fielder. Yelling "hey batter, batter, SWING!", or "he's not a pitcher, he's a belly itcher", is poor sportsmanship; so is yelling "drop it" to the fielder camped under a fly ball. The taunters' goal is to distract and disturb the other team's players.

From the dugout

Block out the noise, and focus on what you're there to do. Distractions in life, like those on the baseball field, can affect the quality and outcome of your performance. Someone is always whispering or giggling in class. E-mails and instant messages bombard you at your desk. The phone, the TV, the digital music player, the online chat room. Your ability to ignore the chatter of life can be the difference between getting it done and having it done to you. When you're up to bat, it's just you and the pitcher; when you're pitching, it's just you and the catcher; when you're in the field, it's just you and the ball. Ignore everything else. Lock in, block out, and get it done.

More from the dugout

Taunting is a special type of distraction—one that is mean and unsportsmanlike. Gossip is a real life example of baseball field taunts. There will always be taunters and gossips in the world—those who feel better when they're embarrassing others. In baseball, the best teams and the best players don't taunt—it's the teams that aren't satisfied with their own performance on the field that taunt the other team. Speak with your actions and your accomplishments, not by heckling. When you gossip, you are finding shallow satisfaction at great cost to others. When you are dealing with gossip that is directed *towards* you, see it as chance to toughen your skin. Know that people who gossip about you are not happy with themselves and hope to make you and others unhappy as well. Block it out. When they taunt "Hey batter, batter", they really mean, "Hey, I wish I was better".

CHAPTER 11

PITCHES

Hitting a baseball is one of the toughest challenges in sports. If human pitchers were just a little more like those pitching machines in the batting cage, it would be a whole lot easier to hit during a game. Machines are consistent and predictable; once a hitter finds where the machine's pitch is going, it goes there almost every time. And once he's adjusted to the speed and angle of the machine's delivery, the batter has seen everything the machine has to offer. But human pitchers are purposely inconsistent; they try to fool the hitter by changing speeds, changing spins, and changing angles on their pitches. Breaking balls mess up the timing of the batter expecting a fast ball. A sidearm delivery confuses the hitter expecting the pitch to come over the top.

From the dugout

Life is not a pitching machine. Life is unpredictable, tricky, and random. Our plans are disrupted, our schedules disturbed, our attention distracted, our sense of order disordered. Don't get upset or panic because of life's spins and angles. Respond as best you can to each new situation or challenge as it comes, adjusting your mind and body to the pitch being thrown. Don't expect to get a hit the first time, and don't expect to get a hit every time. Your first swing may be clumsy or awkward, but learn from it so the next swing is better. Remember that it's just a pitcher and it's just a baseball. A substitute teacher is still just a teacher. A sleepover at a friend's house is still a bed and a pillow. High school is like middle school, except with bigger hallways and kids who shave. College is like high school but with a roommate who's not your brother. A new home in a new town will become familiar and routine if you are patient and willing to adapt to the change. The pitching machine is too easy. Unpredictability and change can make life more interesting, mysterious, and fun.

More from the dugout

Sometimes, though, life throws you a real bad breaking ball. Tragic disruptions of your routines, like your parents' divorce, a grandparent's death, or your own illness, can have devastating effects. And yet, even in these circumstances, you have to adjust so that you can go on. There is no easy way to adjust to tragedy, but you have to stay in the batter's box, stay in the game. Your parents love you even though they are leaving each other. Adjust by seeing the change as doubling the number of loving households. Get through a grandparent's death by finding comfort in the memories you have. Although she won't be there tomorrow, she was there for many yesterdays and you made her happy and proud. If you have a bad illness, realize that your family, friends, doctors, and nurses are all on your team, in the dugout with you—you are not fighting alone. If you can get past the huge adjustments like these, everything else that life throws at you in the future will just seem like a pitching machine.

CHAPTER 12

THE COUNTS

In the classic man-on-man battle between pitcher and batter, the count, or the number of balls and strikes, instantly shows who has the advantage, and who's at a disadvantage. "Working the count" means the batter applying strategy to his at-bat in order to get to a count that's better for him. That involves knowing when to swing and when not to swing. When the batter is ahead in the count, the pitcher has to throw a strike—usually the fast ball right down the middle that the batter is hoping for. But, when the pitcher is ahead, the batter can expect tricky curveballs and pitches too high or too low to be hit well. When the batter is ahead, he can afford to not swing at a pitch unless he really loves it. When the pitcher is ahead, he can afford to "waste" a pitch hoping the batter will swing anyway.

From the dugout

Life is full of counts, some to your advantage, others to your disadvantage. Your goal should be to "work the count" to improve your odds of success. The count is in your favor for getting a "hit" on a homework project due in a week if you start when you get the assignment and finish it early, or pace yourself to finish it on time. The count shifts against you if you wait until the night before the homework is due to start your work. Same with a test. If you begin studying several days ahead of the test, the count's in your favor; wait until the last night and the pitcher (teacher) has you right where she wants you. You never know what's going to come up at the last minute to stop you from studying the night before the test. Going on a date with someone you really like and want to make her like you, too? The count's in your favor if her parents like you and trust you. Show up on time, get back on time, call with any changes. Disappoint your date's parents, the count shifts against you. Applying for a summer job? The count's in your favor if the application form is neatly filled out and you look clean-cut and mature on your interview. The count shifts against you if you make the wrong first impression. Don't let yourself be put in the position where you *have* to swing to avoid the strikeout. Get ahead in the count, so every next pitch is to your advantage, a fastball right down the middle.

More from the dugout

Sometimes you can't avoid having the count go against you—bad calls by the umpire, sneaky pitches by the pitcher, or your own errors in judgment at the plate. When "down in the count", change your approach to hitting—choke-up on the bat, shorten your swing, be less picky, and just try and make contact with enough pitches to make something happen. Off the field, you also have to change your approach when the odds are against you. Don't wait for the home run pitch; instead, make the most of what you're given. Not every swing in life results in a big hit. You may have to aim for slightly lesser goals, settle for slightly worse results than you're hoping for until the count shifts back in your favor.

CHAPTER 13

THE CALLED STRIKEOUT

Strikeouts come in two types—swinging and called. Both are painful for the batter, because he fails to put the bat on the ball. The called third strike, though, is among the most frustrating of baseball's frustrations because it is a failure that comes from standing there and doing nothing. A batter's goal should be to *never* take a called third strike. When there are two strikes, no matter how many balls, the batter has to "protect the plate". Meaning, the batter can't look for perfect or even close-to-perfect—if the pitch is close enough that the umpire *might* see it as a strike, the batter has to swing at it. That means that with two strikes, the batter has to be *ready* to swing, *plan* to swing, and then *swing* at the next pitch unless it is so obviously a ball that even *this* umpire will call it that way.

From the dugout

There are situations in life where another strike would be bad news. At those times, take the risk of going down swinging. If you don't swing, you will probably go down anyway—but if you take the chance, you just might get a hit. When you're down two strikes, learn from those earlier pitches, and try again. Reapply, re-submit, re-request, petition, appeal, try-out again. Admissions committees, coaches, casting directors, talent scouts, and employers often reward those who are persistent and keep on swinging. Life rarely rewards you for standing there and doing nothing.

CHAPTER 14

THE SWINGING STRIKEOUT

Strikeouts from swinging at bad pitches are almost (almost!) as bad as taking a called third strike. But, it happens all the time. The batter who is nervous, or insecure, or impatient swings at everything the pitcher throws at him. Curve balls in the dirt, fast balls above the shoulders, pitches too far outside to reach. The only time a batter should swing at a pitch he doesn't *love* is when there are 2 strikes and the next pitch could be close enough for the umpire to sit the player down. But, until there are 2 strikes, the batter must be picky and patient. Just making contact with a pitch isn't good enough—the batter needs to hit the ball hard and far. To do that, the pitch needs to be one the batter *loves*.

From the dugout

There is no reason to swing at bad pitches off the baseball field either. And you'll have many temptations. People you should-n't hang out with, parties you shouldn't attend, car rides you shouldn't take—these are all curve balls in the dirt that you have to avoid when the count's in your favor. And in life the count is almost always in your favor. It's rare that you'll be pushed into making a bad decision because you're already down two strikes and can't take the chance of letting a pitch go. And if you are in that position, it may be because you swung at earlier bad pitches that got you in a hole. Use good judgment and common sense to avoid the bad pitches. Analyze each pitch, know the count, and know your own abil-ities and limits. Wait for the right pitch, your pitch, the one you *love*, before taking a swing—and then hit it hard and far.

CHAPTER 15

THE CHECK SWING

If the batter starts to swing, and then stops before his wrists bend, the umpire should not call a swinging strike. Checking, or holding up, before fully committing to a swing lets the batter get a head start on his swing, but still gives him an escape for not going all the way. The check swing is used most by two types of hitters: those that are aggressive, hoping to "attack" a pitch and meet the ball well out in front of the plate; and those who have trouble making decisions, not sure when to swing or whether they should be swinging at all. It can be hard for the umpire to tell if the check swing has gone too far, so he often calls it a strike even though the batter tried to hold up.

From the dugout

Some pitches in life come at you fast and right down the middle, others curve and confuse. Even after you've started to respond to a new situation or challenge, it's okay to change your mind if the pitch surprises you or is way out of the strike zone. Realizing that you've made a mistake part way into your reaction shows integrity, honesty, and the ability to think about your own actions and behaviors in real time. It also shows that you're not afraid to aggressively plunge in or, occasionally, courageously back out.

More from the dugout

Changing your mind in *every* situation and after *every* pitch means you have trouble making commitments and keeping promises. Be as careful and thoughtful about your decisions as you can; it should be rare, not routine, for you to change your mind and back out once you've agreed to do something. Commitments are important bonds between you and others; sticking to your promises proves that you are dependable and trustworthy. Remember, check swings are often called strikes because it can be tough for those watching to know if you really went too far before trying to back out. The more you use check swings, the more likely you are to strike out.

CHAPTER 16

DROPPED THIRD STRIKE

When the catcher drops the ball after the 3rd strike, the batter can run to 1st base if there isn't already a runner there. This gives the batter a second chance to get on base and erase the out he otherwise would have caused. In order to get him out, the catcher now has to retrieve the ball and throw it to 1st base before the runner gets there. Hitters often forget this second chance—they are used to just accepting the strikeout and going back to the dugout. After the catcher drops the 3rd strike, the hitter may have already given up and only realizes he should be running to first when he hears everyone else on his team and in the bleachers yelling, "RUN!!"

From the dugout

Your should always try to get it right the first time—be prepared for the pitcher, make good decisions, work the count, don't strike out. But, when things don't work out the first time and you are given a second chance, grab it and run with it. Life often teaches lessons "the easy way", with no harm done, no out recorded. Don't wait for everyone to yell, "RUN". Appreciate when life gives you a second chance after a mistake, and don't make the same mistake again. And then there will be times when *you'll* be in the dugout yelling "RUN!!" as a teammate forgets what to do or loses his way. Someone else's bad experiences are another chance for you to learn. Learn lessons the easy way so you'll never have to learn them the hard way.

 **CHAPTER 17**

THE WALK

Four balls during an at bat earn the batter a "free" walk to 1st base. Many batters, though, hate walks because they would much rather hit the ball. On the other hand, there are those that don't have enough courage or confidence to swing the bat; they go to the plate hoping for a walk. The result is that some players swing at pitches they shouldn't because they are desperate to hit and not walk; and other players don't swing at pitches they should because they hope the umpire will have mercy and call four balls.

From the dugout

The thought of a free walk can hurt those who want it and those who don't. Don't even consider a walk when you go to the plate. Handle each pitch as it comes; swing at the good ones, let the bad ones go. Walks will happen, or not, whether you're dreading one or hoping for it. Sometimes you do get a free pass in life, an easy way out of a tough situation. A lucky break, a happy coincidence, a fluke, perfect timing, a one-in-a-million chance. But if you go to bat expecting a walk and looking for the easy way out, you're likely to strike out waiting.

CHAPTER 18

TAKING A PITCH

After a batter has walked or been hit by a pitch, the next batter up has an advantage over the pitcher who is now rattled by having just put a man on base. Coaches will often tell the next batter to "take" (not swing at) the first pitch after a pitcher's mistake. If that pitch is a ball, the coach may again tell the batter not to swing, sending the pitcher a message that the hitting team is going to wait and see if he can still throw a strike. A couple of balls thrown to this batter after the previous batter got a free pass will further shake the pitcher and may lead to more walks and hit batters, and more base runners and runs.

From the dugout

As unkind and heartless as it may seem, taking advantage of an opponent when they're down, or at least not helping them up, is the way the game is played. This is not a bad thing. Finding a competitive edge is helpful for many of life's goals. Your first strategy should be to make the most of yourself, be the best that you yourself can be. But, knowing your opponent, your competitor, is also important. There is a difference between being a cruel competitor, and being a smart competitor. Not swinging at a pitch from a struggling pitcher forces the pitcher to perform, without you having to cheat or be sneaky or mean. There's nothing wrong with winning at someone else's expense as long as it's done fairly and honestly. In a competition, someone has to win—it might as well be you.

CHAPTER 19

THE SACRIFICE

Whether by bunt or by fly ball, the sacrifice means that a batter purposely gets out in such a way that it advances other runners and helps his team. Even though the sacrifice is not nearly as glamorous as a home run, it is one of the most important skills a hitter can have. The sacrifice only works, of course, when there are less than two outs—otherwise, the out will end the inning and be of no help to the team.

From the dugout

There are times when your own success must be measured by the success of others that you help advance. Sometimes this comes at a significant cost to you, but you'll feel good about your sacrifice even though you may be out—out of the personal time or possessions that you've generously given. And, don't wait until the last minute to sacrifice for others—sometimes, like when there are already two outs, you may be too late. In the words of the famous non-baseball scholar, Hillel: If I am not for myself, who will be for me? If I am only for myself, what am I? And, if not now, when?

 **CHAPTER 20**

THE BUNT

If David had been armed with a baseball bat instead of a slingshot, he surely would have bunted against Goliath. A bunt is what happens when the batter uses his bat to push or punch the ball into the infield, hoping to move up the base runners, or surprise the fielders and reach first base himself. It's a lot easier to judge balls and strikes when bunting than it is with a full swing. The bunter stands almost perfectly still, in a compact position, staring right at the pitcher, and turned toward the incoming pitch. The bunter is not distracted by the usual hitters' routine of stepping and swinging, movements that can make it harder to put the bat on the ball. Bunting can also be the most effective way of dealing with an overpowering pitcher—it is much easier to bunt a heater or a breaking ball than it is to find those pitches cleanly with a full swing.

From the dugout

Bunting gives you a few additional split seconds to focus on the pitch, see the ball, and judge where it is headed. Is it a ball or a strike, a curveball or a fastball? The speed and curves of life often get in the way of your good judgment. Your day-to-day responsibilities and routines can take on a life of their own, overpowering you and distracting you from putting the bat on the ball. At those times, get into a bunting position and give yourself a few extra seconds to find the ball. Drop an activity that's taking up too much of your time. Turn down a night or two out with friends so you can collect yourself at home or get some extra sleep. Unplug, unwind, step back and slow down. Tighten your swing, make your stance more compact, and simplify your movements to get a better view of the pitch coming at you.

 **CHAPTER 21**

SMALL BALL

"Small ball" is a game plan by the hitting team to use frequent or repeated bunting to distract, disturb, and generally confuse the team in the field. Many a big, strong, home run hitting team has been brought down by sly and sneaky small-ballers. One bunt is laid down after another. Fielders misplay the bunts, overthrow the bases in their rush to catch the streaking bunters, and lose track of who's running where. The bases fill one base at a time. Runners advance. Runs score.

From the dugout

Not all big accomplishments in life are home runs. Making step-by-step progress, consistently and reliably moving toward your goal, will often get you there faster than by trying to do it all at once. The top home run hitters usually also lead the league in striking out. While certain times in life do call for a "home run mentality" and swinging for the fences, a steady and controlled approach works best in most situations. The win may be less dramatic, but is still a win; and, your chances of striking out are much lower.

CHAPTER 22

THE SUICIDE SQUEEZE

Not all bunts are created equally—some bunts are more important. In most bunting situations, the batter tries to "bunt a strike", to
bunt only if it's a good pitch so the chances of putting down a
good bunt are higher. Occasionally, though, with a runner on 3rd
base, fewer than 2 outs, and an urgent need to score a run, the
coach will signal the suicide squeeze play, telling the batter to bunt
"no matter what" the pitcher throws at him. As the pitcher begins
his motion to the plate, the runner at 3rd base streaks toward home
plate with no turning back—if the batter *does* successfully bunt, the
chances of the runner scoring are great because of the head start
he had, running without hesitation before a fielder can pick up the
ball and throw it home. But, if the batter *fails* to put the bunt down,
the pitch beats the runner to the plate and the catcher simply tags
out the runner, who has just "committed suicide". This out is not the
runner's fault, and the batter who missed the bunt now has to face
the teammates he let down.

From the dugout

You'll be asked for many favors in your life—even many sacrifices.
In most situations, you'll try your best to help out, and in most situations you'll succeed. But not all requests for help are created
equally. There are times when you *must* succeed because the
effect of your failure would be very harmful or hurtful to people
you care about. At those moments, you have to feel the need of
others as if it is your own need. It may be your brother or sister, your
best friend, or your partner on the science project in school. Your
performance when someone is really counting on you says a lot
about who you are. The circumstances may be difficult ones—
the pitch may be in the dirt or over your head, a curveball or fastball. But this is a suicide squeeze—you have to do everything in
your power to put the bat on the ball.

CHAPTER 23

FAKE BUNTS

Sometimes, coaches will signal their batters to stand in a bunting position, but to then pull back when the pitch is thrown and *not* bunt the ball—even if the pitch is a strike. When the batter takes the bunting position, a chain reaction happens in the field. The infielders all yell "BUNT!!"; the 1st and 3rd basemen charge toward the batter; the 2nd baseman runs to cover 1st base; the shortstop runs to cover 2nd base. And, most importantly, the pitcher often loses his concentration and throws a bad pitch. That's usually the reason for the fake bunt—to throw off the pitcher. Fake bunts are devious and, by definition, a little dishonest. A coach often calls for them with a 3-0 count because he doesn't want the batter to swing on that count no matter where the pitch is thrown. By throwing off the pitcher's rhythm with the bunting stance, and by causing a chain reaction with everyone near the pitcher running around yelling "BUNT!!" in the middle of his delivery, the chances of the pitcher throwing ball four go way up.

From the dugout

White lies are life's fake bunts, devious and a little dishonest, with potentially powerful effects. White lies are usually told with good intentions, to spare someone's feelings, to be sensitive, to try and avoid conflict or criticism. But, instead, they oftentimes backfire, hurting others by causing false hope, mistrust, disappointments, and even dangerous results. When your mom asks, "How was your math test today?", you may say "Okay, I think" even though you suspect you didn't do well—this spares you from having to deal with a bad grade until it's actually official. When your dad asks "Has anyone seen my cigarettes" and you answer "no", you may have protected your older sister from your parents' punishment for now. When your mom asks if there was alcohol or drugs at a party, you may say "I didn't see any" to prevent the next question ("who was using them?") and protect your friends (or yourself!). But, the math test usually makes its way home from school, or at least the report card does. Cigarettes are bad for your sister. And kids using alcohol and drugs will ultimately get caught—or worse. When you "fake bunt" in situations like this, you may think you're doing the decent or considerate thing, and you may even get out of a tight spot—but the chain reaction that happens after a white lie can be very serious.

CHAPTER 24

HIT AND RUN

Most plays by the hitting team are solo acts—a batter hits or a base runner steals. At other times, the base runner has to react *after* seeing the batter's hit. But, in the hit and run play, like the suicide squeeze, two or more players have to act at *exactly the same time* in order for the play to work. At the moment the pitch is thrown, the base runner takes off for the next base and the hitter swings at *that pitch*, whatever and wherever it is. In the successful hit and run, the batter gets a hit and moves the runner farther than he otherwise could have reached on a steal attempt alone. If the batter hits the ball but gets out, the head start of the runner reduces the chances of the double play. And, if the batter misses the ball completely, at least his swing makes it harder for the catcher to throw out the runner.

From the dugout

The hit and run play only works if the hitter is on time, swinging exactly when he is told to swing. If class starts at 7:45 a.m., you're late if you arrive at 7:55. That's like swinging two pitches *after* the hit and run play is called—it doesn't help you or your team. The runners in motion depend on your punctual swing. It is disrespectful to others to assume they will wait for you or that their time is less valuable than yours. When you are always late, those who count on you will stop waiting, and instead find others who can swing the bat on time.

CHAPTER 25

HOME RUNS

The most powerful statement a batter can make is hitting a home run. When a batter powers one over the fence, the player and his teammates in the dugout erupt with excitement. The hitter smoothly cruises around the bases, enjoying the thrill and taking in the moment as he heads for home plate. The runs that score are overshadowed by the *way* that they score. For most players, home runs are rare; some players never hit them. A home run is a milestone—an accomplishment that marks an important step forward in the growth of a baseball player. To hit a home run, a player needs strength and conditioning. He has to combine good judgment in pitch selection, good form and timing of his swing, and good hand-eye coordination to contact the ball right on the sweet spot of the bat. Everything has to come together perfectly for the player, at one moment and in one swing. Although it happens in an instant, a home run follows many hours, sometimes years, of teaching and guidance by coaches who know how to put everything together for the perfect swing.

From the dugout

There are many milestones in your life. Your first day of school, your first night sleeping away from home, your first time driving, your first date, your first job, graduation, leaving for college, getting engaged, marriage, having your own kids. Each of them is a strong statement of how far you've come, and an achievement that depends on many things coming together at the same time. As you reach each new milestone of your life, remember that you have been lovingly, kindly and self-lessly guided there by people who know what it takes to hit one out of the park. As you round 3rd base and head for home in every important milestone of your life, look up in the stands and wave to those special people. Without them, you might never have left the dugout.

More from the dugout

Not every home run swing is perfect and not every home run clears the fence. "Inside the park" home runs happen when a batter hits one far enough into the outfield that he can get all the way around the bases before the fielders get the ball back home. The effect on the score is the same as when the ball leaves the park, but the hitter has no time to smoothly cruise home or take in the moment. He has to streak around the bases, running as fast as he can to beat the throw. You don't reach every milestone in your life exactly the way you planned. Sometimes, the guidance and advice you get isn't perfect, the people along the way haven't been loving and selfless, the swing doesn't come together the way it should, and you're not able to clear the fence and smoothly cruise home. To get where you want to go, you may have to run much harder, making your own path and teaching yourself. But when you hit your "inside the park" home run, you can be very proud that you overcame the hardships on your way and scored despite them.

CHAPTER 26

FOUL BALLS

The first and third base lines define the boundaries of the playing field; anything hit outside of those lines is a foul ball. A foul ball is a near miss; it can be anything from a near miss home run to a near miss strike out. For the alert and aware batter, foul balls are real-time learning. Each foul ball is preparation for the next pitch, a guide to what is right and what is wrong with the hitter's swing. A right-handed batter who fouls to the right is swinging late; he's swinging too early if the foul goes left (a lefty batter is just the opposite—left is late, right is early). A foul ball straight back is a perfectly timed swing, but the batter hit the ball on its lower half—a more level swing may drive the next pitch straight ahead. Each foul ball improves the chances for a successful hit on the next pitch.

From the dugout

Every day you swing the bat at new pitches that life throws you. Some of your swings become perfect hits the first time; other swings are near misses, foul balls that could have turned out better. A near miss is not a failure or an excuse to simply accept the outcome and move on; it's a way to learn, and a chance to improve your next swing. Understand every question you missed on your biology test before starting on the next chapter, so you don't make the same mistakes on the final exam. Ask your teacher why your class project got a lower grade than you had hoped, and do the next project better. If someone else got the spot you applied for, ask how you can improve your application for next time. Unhappy with the advice you gave a friend? Call her back and give her better advice. Forget to do something important today? Write yourself a note so you'll remember to do it tomorrow. Each time you "foul one off", learn from it and correct your swing until you get the hit you want.

CHAPTER 27

BASES LOADED (PART ONE)

Coming to bat with bases loaded stirs the stomach and knocks the knees of many batters. Whatever the game situation, whoever is ahead and regardless of by how much, loaded bases create a completely different state of mind for the batter. Fans, teammates, and coaches are yelling "ducks on the pond", "they're juiced", "a walk's a run", "they're out there for you". Will it be a dramatic hit? A productive walk? Or, an embarrassing out? While more base runners mean more opportunity, they also mean more stress—and the chances for success drop. Batting averages are always lower with bases loaded than with bases empty.

From the dugout

When the stakes are higher, ignore the stakes. Imagine the bases empty, or picture batting practice before the game, and do what you always do. Make the high pressure situation just another situation, like the ones you succeed in all the time. Approach life's bases loaded moments as you approach bases empty—well-prepared and well-practiced—but without the heavy air that comes with "big moments". The "hardest test in your hardest class", the "biggest interview of your life", the "most important performance of your career", and the "toughest competition you've ever faced" are all relative terms—and should all be followed by "so far". There will always be bigger challenges ahead than those today, and today's will seem routine by comparison. If you approach each new "main event" and "major moment" with the same calm and confidence that bring you success in the regular events and moments of your life, the pressure of loaded bases will fade away. You can hit the ball no matter how many runners are on base; it's just another at-bat.

CHAPTER 28

SWITCH HITTING

A few players have the special ability to hit from both sides of the plate—right-handed and left-handed. This gives them extra flexibility; they can hit righty against a left-handed pitcher and lefty against a right-handed pitcher. Hitting from the opposite side that the ball is coming from *may* give the batter a slightly earlier look at the release point of the ball and a better chance of tracking the pitch before he has to swing. But, batting averages prove that almost every switch hitter actually hits much better from one side than from the other—that is, they are really a more "natural" righty or lefty. Yet, they continue to switch back and forth depending on the pitcher's handedness because they can, and because it *might* give them an advantage over the pitcher. The result is that switch hitters often have a worse overall batting average than they would if they always hit from their stronger side.

From the dugout

Just because you *can* do something, doesn't mean you *should*. In life, skills are only useful if they improve the outcome. Making a competitive team doesn't mean you'll be happy leaving your friends on your old team. Being able to stay up and cram the night before a test and pass the test doesn't mean that you wouldn't do better to study for several nights. Having a car that goes from 0-60 in 5 seconds doesn't mean you should ever go that fast. Being quick-witted doesn't mean you should talk back to your teacher, no matter how clever the comment that comes into your head. Because you've jumped your skateboard off the high curb twice, doesn't mean that trying this time from the top of the banister won't land you in an emergency room. Getting into a famous college doesn't mean that it has the right classes or programs for you. Use your skills wisely; otherwise, you're a switch hitter who always strikes out from your weak side.

CHAPTER 29

HIT BY THE PITCH

The hardest thing to watch in a baseball game, for player, parent, fan, and coach, is a player getting hit by the ball. When a batter is hit by the pitch, there are two victims. The batter hurts and is afraid when he comes to bat again, backing away from the plate before a pitch is ever thrown. The pitcher feels guilty and embarrassed for having caused the pain and for giving up a free pass to 1st base. He loses his focus and confidence, resulting in a chain reaction of more bad pitches, walks, balks, and even more hit batters. And, it's not only batters who get hit by the ball—funny bounces hit infielders in the face; outfielders lose the fly ball in the sun and get hit on the head; runners are nailed by thrown balls.

From the dugout

If you don't want to ever get hit by the ball, you can't play the game. For some people, that's a reasonable decision. In life, many otherwise wonderful activities occasionally cause hurt, physical or emotional; so some choose to stay on the sidelines. It takes courage to step back into the batter's box after you've been hit. But you'll be happier and feel better about yourself if you are able to get back in the game—and the sooner the better, before your memory of the pain exaggerates the actual experience. "Shake off" the sting, because the rest of life is too much fun to miss.

More from the dugout

It also takes courage to step back on the mound and pitch again after you've hit a batter, or hurt someone in the other parts of your life. If you're the one who caused the pain, you can't stop living either. Do your best to make up for it, apologize, give comfort and support. And then you need to move on. Dwelling on your mistake, even when it has caused harm to others, makes you lose your confidence and focus. The result may be a chain reaction of more bad pitches and even more damage.

CHAPTER 30

THE LAST OUT

Baseball is a team sport, and no one player alone can win or lose any game for his team. The heroic diving catch doesn't win the game any more than the other outs made in the field that day. The dramatic hit isn't a game winner without the other hits and runs that came before. An error doesn't lose a game—if the game wouldn't have been as close as it was, the error wouldn't have mattered. And the game was as close as it was only because of other situations, involving other players, which could have turned out better. There are 27 batters or runners on the losing team who are called out in a 9-inning baseball game. The last of those outs is a tiny fraction of the total outs made by that team. But, being the last man standing, and then falling, makes a player feel that it is all his fault, that the weight of the loss is all on his shoulders.

From the dugout

Many of life's games are team efforts in which no one player alone can make or break the game. Put your own performance in perspective—it isn't always as important as you or others might make it seem. Usually, you are only in the position to fail *last* because *others* failed earlier, or because your past successes made you the best person to try. It isn't all on your shoulders. You stand on the shoulders of others and others stand on yours. Don't take all the blame for a loss, or all the credit for a win, unless you're playing solitaire—and even then, luck may be the biggest factor of all.

ON BASE

 **CHAPTER 31**

RUNNING TO FIRST

First base is very different than 2nd and 3rd bases. Runners to 2nd and 3rd base have to stop right on the base, or risk being tagged out by an alert fielder. But, a runner to 1st can run straight past the base after stepping on it. The run to 1st is one of the easiest parts of the game to understand. The goal is a clearly marked distance away and the hitter just has to get there as fast as possible, never slowing to watch his hit or stop on the base. Just run like the wind. But, few players do it the right way, because the natural reaction of every hitter is to look and see where his hit went. Did it make it through the infield? Did it take a tough hop? Did the fielder bobble it? When a runner's attention turns away from running he slows down, resulting in outs that could have been hits.

From the dugout

Don't let your attention wander, because that will slow you down. Concentrate on what you're doing. Identify your goal, measure what you need to accomplish it, and run like the wind—straight through, without distractions, until you have safely crossed the base.

More from the dugout

If the ground ball gets into the outfield, the strategy for the runner to 1st changes. Now he has to "round" first base rather than running through it, and look to see if he can possibly advance to 2nd base. How can a runner know which strategy to take—running straight through, or turning and looking towards 2nd base, if he's not supposed to be watching to see where the ball goes? That's the job of the 1st base coach. The coach is the eyes of the runner, telling him to "run through" or to "turn and look". There are times in life to completely rely on your own judgment and feelings, and other times to trust others to guide you in the best strategy to take. Parents, teachers, school counselors, and college advisors are all in a position to help you at key turning points in your life. Set your own goals and run to them like the wind, but also know when you need to trust the eyes and wisdom of the more experienced coaches in your life.

CHAPTER 32

TURN AND LOOK

Although baseball seems to move more slowly and leave more time for thinking than other sports, there are times in a game where quick decisions are made. After a batter hits a single past the infield, his coach will yell "turn and look" as the hitter approaches 1st base. This means that rather than "running through" 1st, the player should "round" it and take a short turn toward 2nd base while locating the ball in the outfield. The runner and his coach now make a quick but careful decision about trying to stretch the single into a double, or trying to reach 2nd on a fielder's error. Without the turn and look, the runner accepts the single and misses the chance to gain the extra base.

From the dugout

Every accomplishment in your life should come with a look toward the next goal. Usually, you have to pause before taking life's next base. But sometimes, with ambition and with a well-prepared mind, you can leap a base or two just by quickly, but carefully looking for an opening to stretch one accomplishment into two. Enjoy each achievement in your life, but always turn and look, thinking about 2nd base even as you celebrate 1st.

CHAPTER 33

LEADING OFF

When a hitter reaches base, his next role is as base runner. The leadoff is the step or two or three that the runner "cheats" off of the base before the pitcher throws the next pitch. The leadoff may be the difference between getting safely to the next base and getting thrown out trying. But, along with the leadoff comes a tradeoff—the risk that the pitcher or catcher will trap the runner off base for an out. Too big a leadoff and the chances of being caught for an out go up. Too small a leadoff and the chances of getting to the next base go down. There are ways that the runner can lower his risk of being picked off of base: watch for clues in the pitcher's leg movement; stand an exact distance from the base to make sure a dive will get him back just in time; and never take his eyes off the ball, even after it's in the catcher's glove.

From the dugout

Life is all about balancing risk and reward. Too much risk can mean great loss; too little risk and no gain. As a runner, you learn the tricks of leading off. You have to also learn the right leadoff strategies for taking risks in life. The right balance will lower the risk of any decision you make, without giving up your chances to move up. Carefully research an upcoming decision; don't rush into the unknown without time to think; talk to others who have faced the same issue; make a list of advantages and disadvantages; lock in the new before giving up the old. And, sometimes, despite being careful and thoughtful, you'll get picked off—it happens to everyone. The pitcher's move to the base may be quicker and sneakier than you could have predicted and you're out. But, not without a valuable lesson that better prepares you to make the next risky decision that comes along.

CHAPTER 34

STEALING

A daring runner can try to run from one base to the next as the pitcher starts to throw the ball to the plate. The catcher then has to try and throw out the stealing runner. Whether a runner gets away with a steal or gets caught trying depends not only on the size of his leadoff and his speed, but also on factors over which he has no control—the delivery of the pitcher, the location of the pitch, the throw of the catcher, and the ability of the fielder to catch the throw and apply a tag. If the situation is just right this time, the steal may be successful and the runner tempted to try again. But, with different circumstances, the next steal attempt may end very differently.

From the dugout

Whether or not you get away with dangerous behavior depends on many factors which may not be under your control. Running across a busy street without a traffic light, fighting the class bully, snowboarding without a helmet, drag racing, sneaking liquor from your parents, trying drugs just once, shoplifting on a dare (real life stealing!). You may get away with it this time, but if you get caught next time or the time after, the results could be terrible. The more times you do dangerous things, the more likely you'll get thrown out. Don't try it the first time, so you won't be tempted to try again.

CHAPTER 35

SLIDING

Baseball sells lots of laundry detergent. At every base except 1st, a runner hoping to beat a throw and "get under" a tag slides into the base. The player slides by dropping to the ground from his running position and thrusting his feet to the base—while moving at nearly full speed. Well done slides end with the runner's feet exactly touching the base, so that he gets there fast and still avoids getting tagged out. Slides aren't needed *every* time a runner moves to another base, but sliding is a simple precaution for any play that might be close. With much to gain and nothing to lose, runners should slide if there's *any* chance it may help.

From the dugout

Buckle your seat belt, double-check the intersection before crossing, proofread your English essay, tie your shoes, check your tires before jumping on your bike, lock the door, review your answers one more time before turning in the Spanish test, use the earpiece to keep your cell phone away from your head. And, yes, don't run with scissors. When there is *any chance* that a simple precaution might help, with no risk, why not?

More from the dugout

Hands-first slides ("diving slides") are a different story. You may like this style because you think it gets you to the base a split-second sooner than the usual feet-first slide; or because a frontward dive is more natural than dropping to your bottom while moving; or simply because flying forward looks cool. But, hands don't wear cleats. Injuries from jammed, broken, and stepped on fingers are common with hands-first slides. While feet-first slides are simple precautions against the risks of overrunning the base and an easy tag-out, hands-first slides are themselves bigger risks than the out you're trying to avoid. Choices you make often involve comparing one risk to another even bigger risk. The risk of being teased by your friends compared to the risk of joining them in a dangerous prank. The risk of your parents discovering you were drinking at a party compared to the risk of not calling them for a ride and driving yourself home. The risk of failing a test compared to the risk of getting caught cheating. Even if it means getting thrown out at base, don't make the risky slide—you'll need your hands for the next game.

CHAPTER 36

FIRST AND THIRD

A special base running situation occurs with runners "at the corners", 1st and 3rd bases, when there are less than two outs. Long throws are usually not as successful as fast runners. In a 1st and 3rd situation, the runner from 1st can often steal 2nd without the catcher even trying to throw him out, because a throw to 2nd would almost certainly mean the alert runner from 3rd would score. This, then, is usually a free base for the runner at 1st. Although teams in the field have "fake throw" plays to try and capture a 3rd base runner who's too far off the base, the smart runner at 3rd will hold his ground until he sees the throw heading all the way to 2nd base before breaking for the plate.

From the dugout

Sometimes life offers a free base for the thoughtful and well-prepared player. Take it. Not taking a freebie isn't a sign of generosity or of humility; it's a sign of being asleep on the base.

More from the dugout

Like the runner on 3rd getting caught off base by a "fake throw" from a sneaky catcher, not everything that looks like a freebie is real. Wait until the situation is clear and safe before making your move to score. There are people out there who will try and trap you with scams, offers too good to be true. Do your research. Make sure the throw is well on its way to 2nd before assuming it's safe to take home; you'll still have plenty of time to score even if you don't break until you're certain it's a safe steal. The run is a sure thing, unless you are too impatient.

CHAPTER 37

FLY BALLS

A base runner has important decisions to make when his teammate hits a fly ball with less than 2 outs. A fly ball that's *caught* is a potential double play if the runner doesn't quickly get back to his base; this is especially risky with a line drive which is caught so fast that a runner has little time to react. On the other hand, a fly ball that is *dropped* may mean that a runner has to immediately run to the next base before the fielder can throw the ball there for a force out. To lower the risk of an out, and improve the chances of moving up, runners practice their fly ball reflexes: they always "freeze on a line drive" to the infield, and "go half way" on a fly ball to the outfield. By freezing, the runner doesn't get far enough away from his base that he can't get back after the line drive is caught. By going half way, the runner watches how the outfielder plays the ball; if it's not caught, the runner can move to the next base with a big head start; if it is caught, the runner can get back to his base with enough time to beat the long throw from the outfield.

From the dugout

With time to analyze and plan, to get advice and find help, you're likely to make the right response to many challenges that come your way. But, circumstances don't always give you the time to fully think things through. You often have to think on your feet and respond on the spot. Practiced reflexes come in handy in those situations. Your friend offers you a cigarette. Another invites you to joyride in his parents' car. Put this pill in your drink, it will make you feel great. Sign onto this web site, you can meet really cool people. What are you afraid of? Don't you trust me? Everybody's doing it! What's wrong with you? Don't be a baby! Don't be a wimp! These are all fly balls and you're the runner. Have a reflex response that lets you do the right thing, sounding confident and cool, without hesitating or stumbling. "No, I'm not interested." "Sorry, not my thing." "Not today, guys, go without me." "Can't, my parents would kill me". Those reflexes show you have spine and guts, and convictions and morals, and that you know the difference between right and wrong. It also tells those around you that there are conditions they have to meet to be your friend.

More from the dugout

It can be embarrassing to stand up to your friends, and you may feel that if you tell them the *real* reason you won't go along it will make you seem nerdy or weak or un-cool. That's okay. Make up an excuse that you think sounds better, anything that gets you out of doing the wrong thing. "I can't, I'm grounded." "I can't, I have asthma." "My cousin's in town and I have to hang with him". "No thanks, I've done it before and it's boring." Practice your reflex response in your mind before the ball is in the air so you don't get caught off base where you shouldn't be, doing things you shouldn't do.

 **CHAPTER 38**

TAGGING UP

Bases are tiny safety zones. A runner's natural reaction when a fly ball is hit to the outfield is to leave his base and run, impulsively and boldly responding to the crack of the bat. But, when a fly ball is caught with less than 2 outs, a runner is only allowed to move to the next base if he *first* tags up, returning to and touching his own base. If a runner doesn't tag up and the fly ball is caught, he can be thrown out for a double play.

From the dugout

Many times in your life you will feel the urge to take bold action—often impulsively, often in anger. Time to tag up. Return to your base before you react. Pause and reflect for a moment in a comfortable and safe place and let the anger or the urge to immediately act cool a little. This brief breather may not change what you decide to do—but delaying your bold move by a few moments, hours or days usually won't change what you hope to accomplish, either. And, if while you're on base, you change your mind about what your best response should be, you avoid the double play of shame and embarrassment that impulsive and angry behavior often brings.

CHAPTER 39

RUNNING WITH TWO OUTS

When there are already two outs, runners on base begin dashing as fast and as hard as they can for the next base at the "crack of the bat". No matter where their teammate's hit goes, and no matter what kind of a hit it is, the runners have nothing to lose by running, no double play if a fly ball is caught. While there's nothing to lose by running, there is often a lot to be gained. The quicker start by runners not waiting to see the hit means they may get farther or even score on a base hit. Force outs and fielder's choices are harder for the fielding team if runners have a head start, increasing the chances that everybody will be safe.

From the dugout

With nothing to lose, and even a slight chance at getting something you want, why not try? If the worst that can happen is that the inning ends with you in motion, the inning would have also ended had you stood still—why not run as fast and as hard as you can and see what happens? Try-out for band even if you think others are better. Apply to a "stretch" college. Submit your writing or painting to a contest. Enter a sweepstakes for a chance at a prize. Ask for something you really want—you may get it! When you find yourself in one of life's no-lose situations, see it as a chance to win.

CHAPTER 40

BASES LOADED (PART 2)

There's only room for one runner on each base. A runner has to always be aware of, and respect, what the runner ahead of him is doing. This is especially true with bases loaded because the chances for force outs and double plays are so great. Runners on 1st and 2nd have to hold their spots until the runner on 3rd runs home, and the runner on 1st can't move until the runner on 2nd moves to 3rd.

From the dugout

At moments of opportunity, be looking ahead not behind. But if you move ahead too fast, without respecting others in your path, you may run right into a double play. No matter how fast or how smart you are, your own progress often depends on the successful progress of those ahead of you. Stay awake and watch what's going on in front of you. And when *you're* the lead runner, remember that others are following and depending on your wise decisions. If you're too aggressive or too hesitant, you may affect the success of others as well as your own.

CHAPTER 41

THE HIDDEN BALL TRICK

Dirty tricks are unusual in baseball—but the hidden ball trick is an exception. With a runner on base, the infielder closest to the runner's base will go to the mound to "confer" with the pitcher. At that time, he will take the baseball, hidden in his glove, back to his position with him. The pitcher steps on the mound, the runner takes his leadoff, and the sneaky infielder runs over and tags the runner out with the baseball. In another version, with a runner on 2nd base, the pitcher fakes a pick-off throw to the shortstop covering 2nd base and everybody pretends that the ball has been overthrown into center field. When the runner "buys" the fake, he takes off for 3rd base and the pitcher tags him out between bases, or throws him out at 3rd. To prevent getting caught by hidden ball tricks, runners should not take their leadoff until they see the ball in the pitcher's hand, and not break for 3rd base until they see the ball thrown past 2nd into the outfield.

From the dugout

Life is always playing tricks on you. Your plans are undone by unexpected and unwelcome surprises. Teachers change dates for assignments and tests. You get chicken pox the day before your big performance. Your bike has a flat. Games are rained out. Flights are canceled. Your computer crashes. Traffic makes you late. Sometimes you can limit the damage of life's tricks by carefully watching the ball—expect the unexpected, and have a back-up plan in place for when life plays a trick. But many times, life's tricks catch you off base and there's nothing you can do about it. Things are not always under your control and life often gets in the way of your best plans. When you get tagged out, learn from it and try not to fall for the same trick again.

CHAPTER 42

THE LAST OUT (PART 2)

When a team is behind and up for their last at-bat, they really need base runners. If losing by only 1 run, the first runner to reach base safely in that last inning is the potential tying run. Getting that first run home sometimes requires risks—trying to stretch a single into a double, taking a big leadoff or stealing a base to get into scoring position. But, when behind by *more* than one run, although the first runner to reach base is still important, more runners are needed. If the first runner doesn't see the big picture and tries to stretch a single or takes too big a leadoff or unwisely tries to steal a base, he risks making the last out before his team has a chance to put the other runners that they need on base. One runner trying to do too much himself can lose the game for his team.

From the dugout

With a major hurdle to get past, it's tempting to try doing it all at once and all by yourself. But you often need the help of others for big accomplishments. You have to be mature and show self-control to avoid risking too much for important goals, especially near the end of the game. See the big picture—your role in the overall game is important, but may not be the most important. Don't make the last out by trying too hard or taking on too much yourself.

More from the dugout

Although a double looks better than a single on your personal stats, getting thrown out to end the game while trying for that extra base only helps the other team. In a team effort, don't focus on your own glory. When you selfishly try to be a hero for your own fame or popularity, you put your team and the whole game at risk.

CHAPTER 43

THE PICKLE

The pickle, when a player is caught in a rundown between two bases, is one of the most exciting plays in baseball. Fielders line up at each end and throw the ball back and forth, chasing the trapped runner, hoping to tag him out before he safely reaches either of the two bases. How did the runner get in this pickle in the first place? Usually by not paying attention and making a mental error—getting surprised in his leadoff by a pitcher's pick-off move, overrunning a base, or trying to stretch a hit too far.

From the dugout

The best way to get out of a pickle is not to get in one. True, it occasionally works out for the best and you either get back safely to where you were or even move up to the next base. But, the anxiety and embarrassment you'll feel while in the middle, to say nothing of the likelihood of being tagged out, are too high a price for the small chance of gaining a base. Pickles in real life also often result from not paying attention. Daydreaming, replaying the past, or looking too far into the future makes you miss life's cues, clues, and opportunities. Stay in the moment, focus on the immediate situation, and don't get caught between bases.

More from the dugout

One of life's most painful and upsetting pickles comes from lying. Getting caught in a lie puts you in a rundown between your parents, your teachers, your coaches, your friends. Sometimes you'll escape and get away with it. Most times you'll be tagged out. In every situation, you'll feel anxiety and embarrassment. The effects of this pickle last much longer than the immediate tag-out—trust is compromised. Everyone who caught you in the lie assumes that you are lying the next time too, putting you in a rundown even when you're safely standing on base and telling the truth.

IN THE FIELD

 **CHAPTER 44**

THE READY POSITION

The ready position is the pose that the fielders snap into as their pitcher prepares to throw the next pitch. The players stand with their legs slightly spread, their arms out in front of them, and their gloves open and waiting for the hit that may come their way. As each fielder sets up in the ready position, he shows that he is awake, aware, and alert—physically and mentally prepared for anything that might happen next. He blocks out all distractions, directs his eyes toward the pitcher and the batter, with his body ready to spring into action.

From the dugout

Looking ready leads to *being* ready. Even if you are the most warmed up and well-practiced player on the field, you should snap into the ready position before every pitch. The ready position focuses your mind and your body on what's immediately ahead of you. In life off the baseball diamond, the ready position takes many forms. Being awake, aware, and alert in class; clearing your desk before starting your homework; making sure you have enough light before sitting down to read; turning off the TV, CD player, and even the phone before studying. The ready position leads to good study habits, good work habits, and fewer errors when handling the ball.

CHAPTER 45

AROUND THE HORN

One of the most curious baseball traditions occurs after a pitcher throws a strikeout, or an infielder makes an out. When there are less than 2 outs and no runners on base, the infielders proudly throw the ball around to each other before the next batter steps to the plate. The catcher or the 1st baseman usually starts the toss around because one of them is holding the ball at the time of the out. The first throw is to the 3rd baseman, who then tosses it to another infielder who tosses it to another, and finally back to the pitcher to face the next batter. Throwing the ball "around the horn" accomplishes two things for the fielding team. The first is a macho "Congratulations!" to themselves. "We just made an out! We're really good! We're really tough! The other team better watch out because we plan on doing it again!" The second, more important effect is a "pep talk" to those infielders *not* involved in making this most recent out, reminding them that they continue to be very important parts of the game and that they have to be ready for action as the next batter steps up to the plate.

From the dugout

You rarely accomplish things entirely on your own. Your success depends on teamwork from those around you who provide support, encouragement, and sacrifice; and their success, in turn, depends on you. When you do well, remember to thank and praise your teammates; toss them the ball and tell them that you couldn't have done it without them. Even if those in your group didn't help with your most recent achievement, you might not have been in position to have made it without their support in the past. By being humble and sharing the credit, you give your teammates a "pep talk" to achieve even greater glory for themselves and for you.

More from the dugout

It's not just the infielders who contribute to the team's success and deserve your thanks and encouragement. When outfielders make a good catch, and especially when they make a *great* catch, the pitcher runs out toward them at the end of the inning, meeting them half way to the dugout, to thank them for their outstanding effort. The pitcher knows that without the support of his great outfielders, fly outs would become hits and hits would become runs. No matter how far away or spread out your support group might be, give them a grateful "high five" when you reach a personal goal.

CHAPTER 46

THE SHIFT

Just nine players have to somehow cover a huge baseball field, so smart and strategic positioning of each fielder is very important to making outs. The usual positions for the fielding team are "straight-away", meaning the center fielder lines up behind 2nd base; the right fielder is behind the 2nd baseman, who in turn is mid-way between 1st and 2nd base; and the left fielder is positioned behind the shortstop, who is mid-way between 2nd and 3rd base. The 1st and 3rd basemen are a few steps inside their foul lines and a few steps behind their bases. These are the positions fielders take when *nothing* is known about the batter. But, when the fielding team has a history for a batter, they may *shift* their spots to try and predict where the batter is likely to hit the ball.

From the dugout

Although past performance is no guarantee of what will happen in the future, if you ignore the past you are guaranteed to fail in the future. History is the greatest teacher of all, and for better or worse, tends to repeat itself. Your growth as a person is based on knowing and learning from your own history and from the past experiences of others. If certain behaviors or relationships have gotten you where you want to go, and others have gotten you or people you know in trouble, shift your conduct and your contacts to take you in the right direction. Don't invite trouble by positioning yourself carelessly and without remembering the past. Hanging out in the wrong places and with the wrong people leads to the wrong outcome; identify those wrong places and people—and shift to avoid them. Knowing where the ball has ended up before should guide you in making decisions; in most cases, the shift you make will put you where you need to be.

More from the dugout

One of the most valuable things you own is your reputation. Your reputation affects how people treat you and whether they respect you. When you are known as someone who is honest and trustworthy, people will shift their treatment of you to show their trust. After you've proven yourself as punctual, dependable, straight-talking, and diligent, people will assume those wonderful qualities about you. A good reputation will outlast the time it takes to earn it. But, the same is true if you've earned a bad reputation. Dishonest, unreliable, uncaring, and lazy are also reputations that are hard to shake; others will assume that you will continue to show those traits, and will shift the positions they take towards you. Your behavior today will affect how people treat you for a long time to come.

CHAPTER 47

THE GROUNDER

Baseballs take funny, sometimes ferocious bounces. Oftentimes the "routine" grounder is the toughest play on the field. An infielder has to center his legs around the fast-approaching ball, and keep his glove right between his legs, low to the ground to prevent the ball from squirting under his glove and into the outfield. Even if the ball doesn't land squarely in the glove, instead taking a funny hop off of the fielder's arm or chest, he may still be able to make the play if he can keep the ball in front of him.

From the dugout

Problems are unavoidable when you let things slip through the cracks. Routine plays in life, details like appointments and assignments, get past you when you don't take them seriously or focus enough on them. Games are lost when the ball squirts under your glove. Being effective in what you do, and being seen as reliable by those around you, depend on your attention to life's little details. Center yourself around a responsibility; keep a list, keep a calendar, write things down. Keep the ball in front of you—right in front of you where you will see it often and remember how important it is.

CHAPTER 48

THE POP FLY

The most dreaded play in baseball, at least for the fans watching in the stands, the pop fly gives players time to run to the ball and camp under it. Too much time. Too many fielders get there at the same time, each looking straight up, gloves ready—followed by the familiar crash, with the ball dropping to the ground between the fielders' writhing bodies. Or, all the fielders yell "mine, mine" as they gather under the pop fly, only to politely back away as the ball falls back to earth; each player waits for the other to make the catch, and then points accusingly when no one does.

From the dugout

Take charge. Often life presents challenges that overlap obvious assignments or clear-cut boundaries. Someone has to step forward, call the ball, and wave everyone else off so there won't be a crash. One voice has to be louder, the leader of that situation. Once you've established that you're in charge, follow-through and try to catch the ball. And then, accept responsibility for whatever happens. Take credit for the good catch, and take the blame for the miss.

More from the dugout

Don't assume anything, and check everything. If you're "calling" for the ball, make sure others hear you; if someone else is calling for it, make sure you hear them. In today's high tech world, you depend on so many ways of communication that it's harder than ever to be certain your message is getting through. Don't assume that someone got your words or note, whether you sent it by land phone, cell phone, text message, e-mail, instant message, on-line chat, message board, postal service or express mail. Just because you sent it doesn't mean they received it. Not everybody reads every message or checks their mailboxes every day. Black holes in cyberspace lose letters and memos all the time; so does the post office. When it's important that your message—or assignment or project—gets to where it's going and gets heard, follow through. Make a phone call, speak to a real person, or get proof by some other route. Otherwise, you've let the ball drop.

CHAPTER 49

SHORTSTOP AND RIGHT FIELD

Everyone thinks that the best fielder on the team plays short-stop, and that the worst plays right field. Shortstop is the "star" position that every talented kid wants to play. On the other hand, right field is seen as the best place, besides the bench, to hide a "lesser star" and minimize his potential harm to the team. Although coaches may assign positions that way, it doesn't make sense. Reviewing the hits in most games shows that as many or even more go to the right side of the field, second base and right field, than to shortstop. The better and faster the pitcher, the later the swings are by the batters, and the greater the chance that hits will go to right field.

From the dugout

If you're put in to play right field, see it as an opportunity, not an insult. The chances of a ball coming to you are greater than you or the coaches may expect—be ready to surprise everyone with your performance. Making the play that no one expects you to make is much bigger than making the play, as a shortstop for example, that everyone does expect. The right fielder is blessed with lower expectations, and therefore lower pressure than the shortstop (and any other position on the field!). The lower the expectations of you, the greater your chance to impress. Become the best right fielder in the league, and be proud of that accomplishment. Become expert at whatever position you're given. You're a specialist! In life, you may not always get your first choice position—but whatever you're assigned, chances are you'll have the opportunity to make a play. Make the most of every opportunity.

CHAPTER 50

FIRST STEP IN, FIRST STEP BACK

When the ball is hit, fielders react quickly and predictably. Infielders "charge" a ground ball, taking their first step *in* and continuing toward the ball rather than waiting for the ball to get to them. This gives the infielder the chance of grabbing the ball on a better bounce. But, when a fly ball is hit to the outfield, the outfielder takes his first step *back* because moving backward is harder than moving forward; it's easier to correct a wrong first step back by running forward than it is to fix a wrong first step forward by running back. The right first step gives the fielder his best chance of making the play.

From the dugout

First impressions are your first steps in new relationships with friends, teachers, bosses, and others. Make the right first impression, and you're off to a good start; the wrong first impression is hard to correct and may send you running backwards to chase a ball that's gotten past you.

More from the dugout

Get off to the right start on every play. Before beginning a new assignment or project, your first step should be to determine how hard it is and how long it's going to take so you can pace yourself. When you're faced with complicated new challenges or offers, your first answer should be, "I'll need a few minutes to think about that", or "I'll have to let you know tomorrow". Before telling someone what you really think of them, take a step back and think about how you'll feel tomorrow when you have to face that person. The right first steps give you a better look at where the ball is going and a little more time to judge the bounce before you try to make the play.

CHAPTER 51

THE STRETCH AT FIRST

First basemen are picked to play that position for a number of reasons; one of the most important is their ability to "stretch". Throws from the infield to 1st base can be long, off-balance, and off-target. The 1st baseman's job is to catch the ball and at the same time keep his foot on the base in order to get the out. The talented 1st baseman can stretch toward the ball, elastic-like, without losing contact with the base. But, he also has to judge when he won't be able to make the stretch. If the throw is too far off target, the 1st baseman has to leave the base and catch the ball wherever it flies to prevent an overthrow that lets the runner move past 1st base.

From the dugout

Reach out to support a friend in need, contribute to a group, make a positive difference in the community. Not everyone can or will make these stretches, but if you do, the rewards are great—those you've helped will appreciate you, those who saw your effort will admire you, and you will feel satisfied and fulfilled. But, you have to also realize when a stretch is too far and you may risk doing more harm than good. In those situations, like the 1st baseman, you need to pull your foot off the base and not stretch further. Friends in trouble may "need you" to cheat, lie, cover up, behave recklessly or dangerously for them. Even if you mean well, those are all stretches that go too far. Know when to reach out, but also know when to pull your foot off the base, so the ball doesn't get past you and cause more damage.

CHAPTER 52

THE DOUBLE PLAY

A double play means that two outs are made on the same play. Double plays can change the character of the game, shutting down rallies and shifting momentum. The two most common types of double play are a fly ball that is caught with a base runner trapped off of his base, and a ground ball to the infield that is quickly fielded and relayed from base to base getting two runners out. The first type is common; the second is harder, happens less often, and results in many errors. The ground ball is misplayed because the fielder is rushing to turn the double play; the throw is hurried and off line; and the relay throw from one base to another ends up in the bleachers.

From the dugout

Everything in its time. Don't try and make too much of every opportunity in life. If the perfect chance for the double play comes your way, go for it, but realize that one out is better than none. If you are too ambitious before you're ready, you may bobble a goal that you could otherwise reach. Sometimes it's better to hold onto the ball than to throw it away, especially when the chances for that second out are low. In other words, the ball in hand is better than the ball in the bushes.

CHAPTER 53

FIELDER'S CHOICE

With runners on base, an infielder has several choices when a grounder comes his way. With less than 2 outs, his top priority is to get out the "lead" runner, the runner headed for the highest numbered base. In the most common example, with a runner on first, the fielder will handle the grounder and toss the ball to second base to force out the runner coming over from first. The fielding team has now made an out without a change in the position of the runners. On the other hand, if there are already 2 outs, the fielder's top priority will be to "get the easy out", meaning he will throw the ball to the closest base where he can get a runner out. In this situation, the fielder increases the chances for a final out in the inning by making the easiest, and safest, play available.

From the dugout

Set your priorities, for the whole game and for each individual situation that may come up. Sometimes, as with 2 outs and runners on base, whatever's easiest is the top priority and you take the safest, surest path to get the job done; get the easy out, and move on to the next inning. At other times, choosing the easiest path might let runners move up, threatening a more important priority; in those situations, you make the harder, longer throw—because what's important is not only getting the job done, but also the effect it may have on your future and the whole game. Know your priorities ahead of time so you'll make the right choice when the ball gets to you.

CHAPTER 54

BASES LOADED (PART 3)

A fielder has many options if the ball comes to him with bases loaded—sometimes too many options. The fielder's position, the number of outs, and the type of hit determine the best play among the many possibilities for that situation. With all those choices to make, with so little time to make them, and with all those runners moving with the crack of the bat, the fielder is often overwhelmed. It's not unusual to see the him blow the play, or cleanly field the ball but then hesitate with confusion long enough that everyone is safe everywhere. More than any other situation in baseball, the fielders in a bases loaded situation have to see into the future. The fielder has to imagine the play happen *before the pitch is thrown*, planning exactly what he'll do if a ground ball, a line drive, or a pop-up comes his way.

From the dugout

Complicated situations are common in life. As with bases loaded, you need to think about the options and picture your responses to tough situations *before* one of them occurs. Friends doing drugs. Your brother getting mixed up with the wrong crowd. Disruptive or disrespectful classmates. Bullying by the school jerk. An abusive uncle or coach. In life situations like this, the bases are loaded and the ball is heading your way. If you haven't pictured the play you're going to make before it happens, you risk blowing it. If the circumstances are overwhelming, find someone to advise you—your parents are the best choice, but there are others who can help—your older siblings, your school counselor, a favorite teacher, your priest, minister, or rabbi. Those you confide in will welcome your trust in them and admire your wisdom and maturity in thinking ahead, avoiding confusion, and making the right play.

CHAPTER 55

CUT-OFFS AND RELAYS

When the ball is hit to the outfield with runners on base, the *infielders* snap into action, too. The throw from the outfield to the infield is long and the base runners are moving fast. To help the outfielder in getting the ball to the right place and limiting how far the runners can go, an infielder will dash part way into the outfield to relay the throw to the appropriate spot. Rather than trying to figure out where all the runners are, where the ball is ultimately supposed to go, and then throwing it there themselves—all in the few seconds after fielding the ball—outfielders can concentrate on cleanly playing the ball. They then just "hit" the cut-off man who is standing in his customary spot. The outfielder who "misses" his cut-off man risks a bad throw that lets runs score.

From the dugout

For the tough jobs, hit your cut-off man. Getting help isn't a sign of weakness or laziness if you are overwhelmed. Rather, it shows that you are realistic and mature enough to know how important it is to get it done and get it done right. If others are already assigned to help you, use their help gratefully and graciously. If you've gotten no help but need it, ask for it politely and respectfully. Know your own abilities and your own limits so the ball ends up where it's supposed to go.

CHAPTER 56

THE WARNING TRACK

At the edge of the outfield, the grass gives way to narrow strip of dirt that runs all the way along the home run fence. This warning track reminds outfielders who are chasing fly balls, with their eyes turned to the sky, that the wall is coming up fast. When the fielder's cleats hit the dirt patch, he knows to slow down or stop running backwards so he doesn't crash. Thanks to the warning track, the ball may hit off the wall, but the player won't.

From the dugout

Warnings protect you from crashing. When you have your focus and attention elsewhere, you may not see the risks or dangers that are coming up fast. Worries about whether you're popular and what you're friends think about you. Imagining what you're missing by "wasting" your time studying. Thinking about how much fun you could have if only there weren't rules and laws. Those kinds of fly balls can get you running backwards with your eyes to the sky, and make you forget that you're coming dangerously close to hitting the wall. When you get a warning, from your parents, your teachers, your coaches, or a forgiving policeman, hear it and obey it; feel your cleats hit the dirt so you don't crash.

CHAPTER 57

ERRORS

There are three types of errors—fielding, throwing, and mental. Fielding and throwing are skills that can be practiced and improved, but never perfected. Mental errors are errors in judgment—throws to the wrong place, running at the wrong time, taking too big a leadoff, swinging at a bad pitch, missing a coach's sign. Errors frequently pile up on top of each other. A fielding error may lead to a rushed and off-line throw. One bad throw can lead to another as runners keep running and fielders keep trying to catch them. Once a fielder has mis-played a grounder, he is likely to misplay the next one hit to him too, because he has lost his confidence and is desperate not to make another mistake. Errors made fielding or throwing are counted and scored because they end up with a runner being at a base that he shouldn't have reached on that play. Mental errors, on the other hand, never reach the scorebook, but they are the most embarrassing of all, and can dramatically change the outcome of a play or an entire game.

From the dugout

As long as human beings are involved, it's impossible to completely avoid errors. One way to measure you as a player, in baseball and in life, is how you react to the error. Do you hang your head, sulk, kick the dirt, throw your helmet, and lose your focus? Or, do you pound your glove with your fist and move on to the next play? Do you lose your confidence and let the errors pile up, or do you tell yourself that was just one play, one mistake, one more opportunity to learn? Do you make excuses and blame others or do you take extra practice to work on the type of play that went bad? Errors may lead to runs scored, games blown, even championships lost. But, tomorrow, the sun rises and another game begins. Errors are lessons learned the hard way, but also opportunities to grow before the next day and before the next play.

More from the dugout

Maintain your focus to reduce mental errors. When you're on the field, the only game that matters is the game on the field. Losing your concentration comes from replaying yesterday's game or last inning's play; or daydreaming about tomorrow's problems or next week's challenges. At important times in your day, block out the past and the future and lock into this particular moment. To this play, this pitch. Be totally involved in the situation right here and right now, focus on it until it's finished, and only then let your thoughts wander off to yesterday and tomorrow.

CHAPTER 58

BACK-UPS

No sport pays more attention to what can go wrong than baseball does, and no other sport so carefully includes back-up into its strategy. For most balls hit or thrown on a baseball field, it is immediately obvious which fielder should be making the play. And yet, almost always, at the moment the ball is in motion at least one and sometimes two other fielders move to back-up the play. They position themselves behind the main playmaker in case the ball gets past him. The ball hit or thrown to third base gets both the shortstop and the left fielder running behind the third baseman to back-up the play. The centerfielder backs up hits to right or left field. The catcher plays back-up on certain throws to first base or third base, and the pitcher backs up throws to the infield and to home plate.

From the dugout

As a fielder, knowing that teammates "have your back" gives you a sense of security and comfort—if you make an error, an alert back-up play can limit the damage. And often it's not an error that causes the ball to get past you—bad hops are part of the game. Just as you get peace of mind knowing that someone is behind you, you have to be there to back-up others. The baseball field is a community of nine citizens, each responsible for the other. In the larger communities where you live, you are also responsible for others. Giving and collecting charity, feeding the hungry, finding or building shelter for the homeless, supporting the disabled, and defending those who are discriminated against are ways for good teammates in the community to provide back-up and prevent the ball from getting past. Because bad hops are part of the game of life, too.

ON THE MOUND

 **CHAPTER 59**

THE MOUND

Rising up from the center of the otherwise flat infield, the mound is the pitcher's "platform" from which he delivers his best stuff. This elevated lump of dirt gives the pitcher an advantage, letting him throw downhill. From the mound, his fastball has more force and momentum and his breaking ball has more room to break.

From the dugout

When you feel strongly about something important, even if you are alone, stand up for what you believe. It may be easier to avoid attention and shrink away from tough positions—which is okay if the issue or problem is just not that important to you. But when it matters to you, don't slink away with the others to flat ground where your voice is harder to hear. Climb up on the mound, take the podium, take center stage. Find a platform to deliver your best stuff; send your message loud and clear, with force and momentum. Know what you stand for and stand tall for it.

More from the dugout

Pick your battles carefully. If you try to take the mound for every opinion or idea that you have, or every time you disagree with someone, people won't take you seriously when something comes up that is especially important to you. Your platform should be saved for the times that you really need it. Then when you take center stage, people will listen.

CHAPTER 60

LEFTIES AND RIGHTIES

Handedness is a big deal in baseball. Left handed pitchers are brought into the game in important situations to pitch to left handed batters. Switch hitters bat lefty against a right handed pitcher, righty against a lefty pitcher. Lefties play first base and outfield, but rarely if ever play catcher, 2nd base, shortstop, or third base, whereas righties play all field positions—unless a left handed player on the same team can play first base, in which case the right handed first baseman usually sits. Explanations for these hand biases, range from the batter having a better view of the pitch from one side of the plate, to the best body angle for a fielder to make a throw or a tag. Really, though, many of these are just *underhanded* myths. Most good pitchers have as much success against opposite handed batters as they do against the same-handed, and good batters hit same-handed pitchers as well as those pitching from the other side. And when given the chance, lefties usually do just fine in the infield, and even play well at catcher.

From the dugout

Stereotyping leads to prejudice and discrimination, and to missed opportunities to play certain positions in baseball and in life. When how you feel about people and what you expect of them is based on their handedness—or their gender, race, religion, physical appearance, wealth, or family background—you are taking away their individuality, their right to be judged as a person rather than as a member of a group. It's not their handedness, but your even-handedness that is most important.

More from the dugout

On any day, and in any game, any lefty pitcher may strike out a right handed batter—or not. A right handed player may be a much better first baseman than a lefty—or not. It all depends on the individual himself, not the handedness group he's in. When you assume things about people, without getting to know them, you're usually wrong—for two reasons. First, the group stereotype itself is likely to be false; for example, lefty pitchers are not necessarily more effective against lefty batters. And, second, even if there is a sometimes true relationship between a characteristic and a group, that doesn't at all predict that any individual in that group will share the characteristic; for example just because most right handed 2nd basemen have a quicker throw to first, any individual lefty may be an all-star 2nd baseman. Don't assume anything about people until you get to know them as individuals.

CHAPTER 61

RITUALS

Baseball is rich in rituals. Every pitcher has his own special rituals, patterns of movement leading up to his pitch, a fingerprint that makes him different from other pitchers. Some kick the dirt twice, tug on their sleeve, hold the ball behind their back leg. Others spit, twirl the ball in their hand while looking in for a sign, push the ball deep in their glove. Some stoop slightly before winding up. Others just send the batter an evil stare. These routines, repeated with every pitch, are not for the entertainment of the fans (although they can be very entertaining!). Rather, they steady, calm, and center the pitcher, making his delivery more consistent from pitch to pitch. By following the same pattern before every pitch, the pitcher hopes to rise above the circumstances of the game, the pressure of the count, and the noise of the crowd. The ritual tells his brain, "this is just another pitch, like the ones before and like the ones to come; I know how to do this."

From the dugout

Tough circumstances, pressure, and the noise of life can throw you off your game. New challenges often require new strategies and new hurdles may need a new approach. But you can find stability in your routines and rituals. As you prepare to face new and difficult problems, kick the dirt a few times. Rely on patterns that calm and steady you before you take action. Get a good night's sleep. Take a shower to open your eyes in the morning. Spend the time to eat a healthy breakfast. Check your calendar to see what you have planned, but don't assume the day will go as you planned. Leave the house on time. Get help and advice from people you trust. Say a little prayer. These are rituals for the real world, routines that help you rise above the circumstances of the game. The problems may be new, but trust your old and reliable routines to center and stabilize you. You know how to do this; it's just another pitch.

CHAPTER 62

DEEP BREATH

Among the most common and useful of a pitcher's rituals and routines is the deep breath, a calm moment of peace and quiet, he takes before every pitch. When swept away by the emotion, pressure, nerves and noise of the moment in a big game, the deep breath helps the pitcher block out the outside world just long enough to focus on throwing a strike.

From the dugout

A moment of peace and quiet can help you through many of life's stressful situations. A deep breath helps you remember the answers on the big test and your lines for the school play. It steadies your voice before you give a speech and relaxes your muscles before you touch the piano keyboard or sweep the bow across the cello strings. Your body even takes deep breaths on its own—a yawn is a subconscious deep breath, filling your body's need for a brief burst of extra oxygen. A conscious deep breath at stressful times of your day refreshes you, calms you, focuses you, and prepares you for what you're about to do.

More from the dugout

Your most relaxed and energizing breaths come during sleep, when your breathing pattern slows and deepens. Everyone needs at least 8 hours of sleep each night; some need 10. People who say they need less sleep are kidding themselves, and cheating themselves. Everything you depend on when you're awake, from your mental alertness to your physical coordination, depends on getting enough sleep. You will pitch faster, hit stronger, and field better with 8 hours of sleep. Your toughest subjects in school will seem easier, and your homework will go faster. You will be more creative and interesting, a better friend and teammate. Don't miss the chance to have a full night of deep breaths.

CHAPTER 63

THE WIND-UP

Most pitchers prefer to pitch with a full wind-up rather than from standing still in the "stretch" position. The pitcher's wind-up uses momentum from his whole body, uncoiling and lunging forward towards the batter, to launch the pitch faster and harder than he can with his arm motion alone from the "stretch".

From the dugout

Use all of your talents and skills to reach your full potential. You may go far with charm alone, but you'll go farther when you combine your winning personality with preparation and study. You'll do well with your brain power, but you'll do even better when you add ambition and enthusiasm. Looking sharp makes the right first impression, but then you make important next impressions by your dependability and integrity. Make the most of the strengths you have now by developing new strengths. Use everything you've got to launch yourself forward.

CHAPTER 64

CHECKING THE RUNNER
(THE STRETCH)

With runners on base, the pitcher can't use his full wind-up motion because it takes a little longer and makes it easier for base runners to steal bases. Instead, he stands straight up in the "stretch" position, first looking over his shoulder at the runner, and then quickly pitching without using more than his arm movement and a short step to the plate. The look over at the runner on base "keeps him close", preventing him from taking too big a leadoff and making it harder for him to steal a base. Runners can't do harm if they're not allowed to move on to the next base. But if the pitcher is careless and forgets to check the runner or accidentally uses a full wind-up, bases are stolen, runs score, and the situation can get quickly out of hand.

From the dugout

Batters will reach base, but how the game turns out depends on how far they get around the bases. Situations in life can go quickly from bad to worse if you don't pay close attention to them. You can usually recover after forgetting one homework assignment, bombing one test, oversleeping one class, or making one trip to the principal's office. But you have to keep those runners in check, not letting them move to the next base. If you're careless, problems multiply and games can be lost.

CHAPTER 65

PICK-OFFS

If at first a team doesn't succeed in getting a batter out, they can try, try, try again. When a runner takes his leadoff, the pitcher can throw over to the runner's base *before* the next pitch, hoping to catch him off base. Or, the catcher can throw to the runner's base *after* a pitch if the runner hasn't returned to base quickly enough. If the runner is tagged out by the fielder covering the base, he has been "picked off" and is out. Pitchers and catchers love to try picking runners off—it fixes the unfortunate events that let the runner get to base in the first place. But, successful pick-offs are rare. That doesn't prevent pitchers from trying, and trying, and trying again, each time they allow a runner to reach base. The more times a pitcher throws over to the base, the more likely it is that one of his throws will get past his infielder, letting the runner happily move on to the next base.

From the dugout

You can't fix all of your mistakes, and sometimes trying too hard to fix them causes more mistakes and more harm. As badly as you might feel about the way something you did turned out, over-reacting and over-correcting can make things worse. Speeding doesn't fix oversleeping; cheating won't make up for poor studying; more lies don't correct the first lie; more gambling rarely wins back what you lost. When you've already let the runner reach base, it's usually too late and often too risky to try correcting that mistake. Sometimes, you just have to accept the result of your actions, learn from it, and not make the problem worse by trying too hard to fix it.

CHAPTER 66

STRIKES AND BALLS

The best pitchers are the ones who most consistently throw strikes. This may seem obvious, but in fact it's often the flashy and showy pitchers, the ones who throw the hardest or who have the trickiest breaking ball, that get the most attention and the most pitching time. When the blazing fast ball pops the catcher's glove for a strike that the batter could barely see, much less hit, the excitement rises on the field and in the stands. The curveball that looks like it's heading straight toward the batter's head but, at the last minute magically dives into the strike zone, draws oohs and ahs. But over the course of a whole season, it's the pitcher who can get the ball into the strike zone most *consistently*, walk and hit the fewest batters, and throw the fewest wild pitches that wins the most ballgames—even if his pitches aren't the fastest or the fanciest.

From the dugout

Consistency consistently beats frills and flare. Occasional outstanding accomplishments are thrilling, but it's the daily, weekly, monthly, and yearly "above average" performances that get good grades, acceptances at good colleges, good jobs and promotions. You should aim for reliable and steady quality rather than for bursts of brilliance. With that realistic goal in mind, a surprising thing will happen—your "above average" performances will become "outstanding" over time. Consistent strikes will develop into consistent fastball strikes and consistent curveball strikes, fast and fancy.

CHAPTER 67

PASSED BALLS

Pitches that should have been caught but get away from the catcher often let runners move up to the next base or even score while the catcher fetches the ball. With runners on base, the catcher has to "be a wall", blocking every pitch he can't cleanly catch so that it stays in front of him and keeps the runners in place.

From the dugout

Life is full of missed opportunities. Although not every pitch is easy to catch, you have to try and prevent the important ones from passing you by. You may not feel ready for the big audition day, or you might be too busy for the volunteer work you promised, or you may have too much homework on the night the college representative is speaking, or you may have just found out about the application for a summer job the day before it's due. These are tough pitches to catch—but if they get passed you, it could change the way the whole game turns out.

CHAPTER 68

PAINTING THE CORNERS

A skillful pitcher can throw to the corners of the plate where strikes are harder for the batter to hit than when they're "right down the middle". Umpires aren't always very strict with their strike zones, meaning that even pitches "off the corners" may be called strikes—as long as they're not too far off. Strikes on the corners are more subtle and trickier than those thrown right down the middle—and safer for the pitcher. By painting the corners with his pitches, a pitcher gets what he wants, strikes and strikeouts, without running the risk of giving up a big hit.

From the dugout

There are many situations in life where being subtle and a little tricky is better than being blunt and bossy. A gentle approach often works best: nudging people in the right direction rather than shoving them there; guiding rather than forcing; hinting, not nagging. Temper tantrums are rarely as effective as calm, logical discussions. Threats cause tension, but compromises comfort. Commands and orders may make people resent you, but suggestions and recommendations show that you respect others and make them more likely to respect you. Try requesting what you need rather than demanding it. Knowing when to throw it right down the middle and when to paint the corners can make a big difference in what the batter does with your pitch.

CHAPTER 69

FRAMING THE PITCH

The strike zone is small and getting the pitch into it can be tough. Many pitches miss the strike zone, either purposely by a pitcher ahead in the count or accidentally by a pitcher off his mark. Too high or too low, inside or outside, catchers will "frame" the pitch, catching the ball while at the same moment sweeping their glove into the strike zone, trying to convince the umpire that the ball was there all the time.

From the dugout

See the best in people that you care about. Put them in the best light, helping them feel better about themselves and look better to others. No one is perfect, but everyone has good qualities and has done good things. If your sister applied to ten colleges and was turned down by six, tell the world about the four where she was accepted, not the other six. If your brother didn't make varsity, help him feel proud about playing junior varsity—lots of people don't even have the guts to try out and end up not playing at all. Instead of teasing a friend about her flaws, help her hide them so others don't see. Disguise the embarrassing moments and mistakes of the important pitchers in your life so that when they blow it, they don't show it to the outside world. Frame their pitches so everyone sees strikes.

CHAPTER 70

THE FASTBALL

For most pitchers, the fastball is their "go-to" pitch, the one they throw with most consistency, accuracy, and predictable results. When a pitcher really needs a strike, especially when he's behind in the count, the fastball is usually his choice. The fastball is simple—no fancy arm motion or mysterious grip. Just rear back and throw the ball hard and straight, right over the plate. Although it's true that most batters prefer to hit fastballs, most fastballs result in strikes that aren't hit.

From the dugout

In most situations, when you really need a strike, you should go with your strength, whatever has been the most reliable approach for you in the past. Nothing fancy or mysterious. Be comfortable with who you are, don't pretend to be someone you're not. If you lose with your best stuff, you'll move on and try again. But, more often than not, you'll win using your most direct and simple pitch—being yourself, and doing what you do best.

CHAPTER 71

THE CHANGE-UP

When a pitcher has a good fastball, another pitch that comes in just a little slower, but otherwise looks just like his fastball, can be a very effective weapon. Batters adjust to a pitcher during the course of an at-bat and from one at-bat to the next. When the pitcher is able to get the batter used to seeing fastballs, and then throw an identical-looking pitch but slightly slower, the results are, well, striking. The batter swings for the pitch he expected, but the ball isn't there yet, and the swing is off target and way "ahead of the pitch", resulting in a strike and often making the batter look silly.

From the dugout

Spontaneity is life's change-up pitch. As valuable as predictability is, an unexpected twist once in a while can add fun, spice, and mystery to your everyday routine. This is true in relationships with friends and family, and even just to keep yourself excited and challenged. While it's often difficult to deal with drastic "curveballs", a subtle change of pace can be refreshing for you and those around you. Clean your room without being asked. Plan a surprise party for a friend. Hug your sister. Write a thank you note. Do the extra credit assignment. Do your laundry. Send a Valentine card. Take a knitting class. Bring your mom flowers. Predictable is good, but too predictable can be boring. If all you throw are fastballs, the batters will quickly figure you out. Change-up once in a while.

CHAPTER 72

THE CURVEBALL

The magic and mystery of the curveball is that it starts out look-ing like one thing and ends up looking very different. When the pitcher dramatically twists his arm and snaps his elbow, the result is a pitch that arcs its way diagonally from high to low and from one side of the plate to the other. The effect on the batter can be devastating as he swings at a pitch that looks like a strike, only to see the ball dive to the ground before ever crossing the plate. Or, he ducks out of the way of a pitch that looks like it's going to hit him in the head, only to hear the umpire call "Strike!" as the ball breaks across the plate.

From the dugout

When you start out looking like one person and end up looking like another, there may be devastating effects on those around you. Daily upsets, mood swings, acting out, and personality changes can be part of growing up—but they can also be part of a more serious problem. If you react to the challenges of life by yelling at your parents and siblings, not coming home at night, talking back to teachers, skipping school—those are all curveballs, hard for others to understand and deal with. Dramatic snaps and twists from your usual behavior affect more than just you. Family who trusted you and friends who depended on you may be hurt and disappointed and may duck out of the way. If you are depressed, angry, and bitter, or feel the world has turned against you, don't throw curveballs at those who love and care about you; get their help. They will be relieved that you came to them, and it's now, more than ever, that you need them.

CHAPTER 73

THE PITCHOUT

When the pitcher and catcher strongly suspect a base runner will be stealing on the next pitch, they may scheme to catch the runner by using a pitchout. As the pitcher begins to throw, the catcher will stand up tall and move to the far opposite side of the batter's box from where the batter is standing. The pitcher throws the ball to his catcher who then has a straight shot at throwing the runner out, not slowed by the usual obstacles of his crouched catching position or the batter's swinging bat. The pitchout is automatically called a "ball" by the umpire; it only works when the pitcher is ahead in the count and another "ball" won't result in a walk or other significant advantage to the batter.

From the dugout

There are obstacles in the way of almost every goal you set for yourself. Like the pitcher behind in the count, you usually have to deal with those obstacles directly and can't avoid them with a pitchout. Rules and requirements, paperwork and deadlines. No way to step around those; just get them done quickly and efficiently so you can move on to the next step. But, other obstacles *can* be avoided. Friends who have ideas for your time that keep you from doing what you should be doing. Distractions that pop up on your computer screen or cell phone. The television or video game machine. Having the wrong supplies, books, tools or equipment for the job you have to do. Those are easy obstacles to get around. Pitchout. Step away from those obstacles so you have a clear view of where the ball has to go.

More from the dugout

Other obstacles come from inside of you. Doubt or insecurity about yourself, shyness, fear of change, worry about the unknown. When you feel these, you're crouching like the catcher behind the plate. The only way to move forward is to realize what it is about you that is keeping you down. Be confident in yourself and in your abilities. The more you do anything the better you'll be at it. Step away from the safety and comfort of old ways and old habits. The worst that can happen if you try something new is that you won't like it, or may even fail at it—you can always go back to the old way. You were only able to discover who and what you now like because you had the courage in the past to meet new people and try new things—imagine all the people you still haven't met, and all things you still haven't tried, that you might like even more. Stand up tall, don't crouch behind your inner obstacles. Now, make a strong throw, a straight shot at your target.

 **CHAPTER 74**

THE INTENTIONAL WALK

There are times in a game where a batter is so much more dangerous at the plate than he would be as a runner on first base, that the pitching team decides to purposely pitch four balls to walk him. By "pitching around" this particular hitter, home runs may be avoided and potentially easier outs or double plays created on the base path. Making the wrong decision and pitching to this batter may lose the game.

From the dugout

You know which situations in life are potentially the most dangerous and should be "pitched around", avoided to minimize the risk. The wrong friends. The wrong prank. The wrong advice from the wrong people. The wrong party. The wrong part of town. The wrong driver. The wrong speed. Make the right decisions. Intentionally walk away from situations that may lose the game for you.

CHAPTER 75

MEETINGS ON THE MOUND

When the game is going badly or when the pitcher is facing a complicated situation, the catcher, infielders, coach, or all of them together may gather on the mound to give advice and strategy. Sometimes there are specific suggestions for the pitcher to work on; other times the meeting is just to calm the pitcher and help him get his control and composure back. The visit to the mound almost always leads to the pitcher throwing better pitches and more strikes.

From the dugout

It can be hard to see the big picture when you're standing in the center of it. The tension and pressure of the game, with runners leading off base, batters staring you down, and fans screaming both for and against you, make it difficult to perform your best. Let in others who have your interests and well-being at heart, and be open-minded to their help and advice. Your parents, teachers, coaches and older brothers and sisters have experienced the same kind of situations and have been in equally tough places. They understand what you're facing, how important, or unimportant each pitch really is, how meaningful or meaningless the outcome of the game really is, and how best to respond to the stress of the moment. If you welcome others to the mound and listen to what they have to say, you'll throw better pitches and more strikes.

CHAPTER 76

THE PITCH COUNT

The more pitches a pitcher throws, the more fatigued his arm grows, the less effective his pitching becomes. Every pitcher has his limits, after which he risks the outcome of the game, and the outcome of his pitching career—going above reasonable pitch counts can cause permanent damage to a pitcher's arm.

From the dugout

Know your own limits. Everyone has physical limits, as well as mental and emotional ones. Pushing yourself *too* hard for personal satisfaction, or for the good of others, or to make up for a previous failure can do permanent damage. Those depending on you may also try to push you beyond your breaking point, hoping to squeeze out just another drop of your ability and skill, or a few more hours of your time and energy. Know when you are reaching your limits, when doing more or trying harder will stress you to an unhealthy level. When your pitch count climbs too high, stop pitching. Protect yourself for the next game.

CHAPTER 77

RELIEF PITCHERS

Every game has a starting pitcher, but few games end with the same pitcher as they started. Relief pitchers usually enter the game when there's already trouble, with big league pressure on their shoulders—runs in, runners on base, lots of walks, best hitters coming to the plate. Relievers are expected, with brief warm-up, to shut down the other team's rally and get their own team off the field with as little harm done as possible. The high stakes change everything; every pitch seems more important, every mistake feels more damaging. Even though it was the previous pitcher that made the mess, the relief pitcher is expected to fix it.

From the dugout

You can only do so much. When you're brought into the game with bases loaded and no outs, chances are runs will score. When the odds are steeply stacked against you, chances are you'll fail. It's tough to win in no-win situations. Do everything you can to save the day—but go easy on yourself if the game is lost. If it had been an easy save, your team could have stayed with the last guy or brought in somebody else. Putting you in the game meant people had faith that you might be able to pull one out; failing this time means that you're only super-human some days, not every day. You may feel as if you let everyone down—but really, it was all the events before you arrived on the scene that let everyone down. And those events were caused by people who may now seem to be the most disappointed in your performance. In their hearts, though, they are really disappointed in their own performances. Most importantly, don't be shaken or rattled. You'll be called on again and you've got to have the confidence in yourself that the next time you may beat the odds and win the no-win situation.

CHAPTER 78

THE BALK

There are strict rules for how a pitcher can and cannot move before he throws a pitch. Those rules protect a base runner from being thrown out during his leadoff by a pitcher who fakes a pitch and then throws over to the base. If the pitcher makes an illegal movement, committing a balk, base runners get to automatically move up a base. A balk occurs with great drama—the umpire screams "BALK!!" in the middle of the pitcher's delivery. And umpires *always scream* when calling a balk. The pitcher is shaken by the scream and embarrassed by the mistake; he then has to watch helplessly as each base runner gets a free base. And then, the rattled pitcher has to make another pitch! After a balk, pitches are usually out of the strike zone and wild. The chances are high that a balk will be followed by more balks, by batters being walked, and by batters hit by a pitch. Pitchers have trouble bouncing back from "balk shock", often leading to more damage than from the balk alone.

From the dugout

"Balk shock" is like many of life's unwelcome screams. In the middle of your daily routine, you may make a wrong move and you hear it: "you're grounded!" or "deadline!" or "too late!" or "pop quiz!" or "to the principals' office!" or "not good enough!" Screams in life, even quiet screams, upset your plans, make you doubt yourself, mess up your rhythm, and throw you off your game. Your next move after the scream is likely to be wild and may cause more damage. When "balk shock" happens, remind yourself that this is just one mistake in an otherwise well-pitched game. You made a wrong move and the runners moved up, but now another batter is at the plate, another chance to do it right. The best way to prevent another balk is to go back to your routine, to the movements that have been successful for you in the past. Limit the damage, regain your confidence, and take back control of the situation. The next time the umpire screams, it will be "Strike 3!" as you've stepped up and gotten out of a tough situation.

CHAPTER 79

BASES LOADED (PART 4)

Among the toughest situations for a pitcher is when the bases are loaded. With all those runners on base, almost anything that happens next can score runs: a base hit, a walk, a passed ball, a wild pitch, a fly ball, and even a ground ball out. Pitchers often react to bases loaded by fearing the worst, and their pitches show it. Pitchers' arm motions change, they over-throw or they aim; their usually reliable pitches miss their mark, and runs score. But, bases loaded also gives the pitcher's team the most options for making outs—force outs can be made at any base and double plays can end the inning.

From the dugout

When you're the pitcher and the bases are loaded, you can choose to be pessimistic or optimistic. On the one hand, the outcome can be terrible; on the other hand, with the right bounce, things may end up even better than they would have with fewer runners on base. Fearing the worst often leads to changing how you act in such a way that makes your fears come true. You can be too careful, too hesitant, too nervous, and too worried about what may happen next. Be optimistic, not pessimistic. Imagine the best possible outcome instead of the worst. You may end up being disappointed, but you will give yourself the best chance for ending the inning the way you hope.

CHAPTER 80

THE PERFECT GAME

A pitcher's greatest achievement is to pitch an entire game without giving up a hit or a walk or hitting a batter. Through a combination of strikeouts and fielding outs, the pitcher faces the other team's best hitters and worst hitters, switch hitters and pinch hitters, letting none of them reach base. Perfect games are extremely rare, and most pitchers will never throw one. In a perfect game, the pitcher makes all the right choices; which pitches to throw to which batters, and when. With each new batter, and with each count on that batter, the pitcher has to choose between fastball and change-up, curveball and slider, down the middle or on the corner, inside corner or outside corner, high or low. Many choices to make, one right after another. One wrong choice and the perfect game may be blown. The pitcher can't possibly make all those choices by himself; he trusts his catcher to help him all along the way. The catcher serves as the pitcher's "conscience", telling him which pitches are right and which are wrong for each situation, sizing up the batter, moving the target, framing the pitch. The perfect game is as much the catcher's triumph as the pitcher's.

From the dugout

In your life, each day brings many choices that you have to make, one right after another. Some of the choices you make have little effect on the game, but others can make all the difference between winning and losing. The choices can be as simple as what to eat for breakfast, and as complicated as whether to join your friends in doing something you know none of you should be doing. Your conscience is your best guide to the tough choices. You know what's right and what's wrong. You've been taught well by your parents and teachers; you have your own past experiences to draw on; and, you have

The On Deck Circle of Life

seen the results of the choices that people around you have made. Listen to your conscience to pick your pitches carefully.

EXTRA INNINGS

CHAPTER 81

HOME FIELD ADVANTAGE

Every team would rather play on their home field. The well-known slopes and valleys in the outfield, the funny lumps and pits in the infield, the familiar nooks and crannies in the dugout, and the friendly faces on the bleachers all give the home team a big advantage over the visitors. Home teams also get to bat in the "bottom" of each inning, which means they have the last chance to score runs at the end of a game. Sometimes, it even seems that the umpire's calls favor the home team. With the comfort and stability of home field advantage, teams almost always win more games at home than "on the road".

From the dugout

As life challenges and confuses you, take comfort in, and take advantage of, your home field. Your parents and brothers and sisters are your best friends, your most important teammates. At times, it won't feel that way. You may think that sharing a secret with your parents, or confessing to them, will only make things worse. It may feel like your brothers and sisters are ganging up against you. You may believe that your friends at school care more about you, judge you less, understand you better, and would certainly never punish you. It is true that parents can act more like umpires, and siblings more like the other team. But that's just an act. An umpire doesn't worry about you, guide you, protect you or love you. The other team doesn't share life's experiences with you, trust you with secrets, or stick up for you in a crunch. No matter how bad the crisis, how afraid you feel, or how terrible you imagine the outcome, your family is your ultimate home field advantage. Find the comfort and stability of your familiar dugout and the friendly faces on the bleachers. You'll win many more games at home than on the road.

CHAPTER 82

THE HEAD TRIP

So many situations in a game affect a player's mind, which in turn affects how his body plays. Umpires' bad calls, walks, balks, hit batters, a close score, angry coaches, bases loaded, loud fans, and errors. When the stressful events of the game are made even worse by the player's own emotional reactions, a head trip occurs. The player over-thinks, over-analyzes, and is over critical of himself. The result is that he underperforms and underachieves. He stomps his feet, shakes nervously, talks to himself, curses at himself, slams his bat, throws wild pitches, throws his glove in anger. None of those reactions improve the way he plays; they pile on and pile up, usually making the head-tripping player useless for the rest of the game. Entire careers have ended for some players who were never able to control their head trips.

From the dugout

Your mind is very closely connected to your body, and your emotions have a big effect on your performance. When you let what's going on around you change how you feel about yourself and about your abilities, you become useless for the rest of the game. You are your own worst critic—but can also be your own best supporter. You can talk yourself up, or talk yourself down. If things are going badly for you or around you, piling on by criticizing or getting mad at yourself will only make the problems worse. Instead, convince yourself that the situation isn't your fault or, if it is, the lessons you learn will help you do better next time. It may be the end of the game, but it isn't the end of the world. You will improve your performance and get through tough situations if you can avoid the head trips. Head trips can end very badly, with lost games, lost seasons, lost futures. Or, you can end them before you let them start.

CHAPTER 83

THE UMPIRE

Being an umpire must be one of the most depressing jobs on earth—maybe that's why they wear blue. Deciding between balls and strikes, safe and out, fair and foul naturally pleases half the crowd and angers the other half. The angry half always argues, loudly, but the umpire's call never changes. At least he gets paid for the abuse. For the players, blaming the umpire for the outcome of their at-bat, steal attempt, pitching performance—for the outcome of the game itself—is the number one pastime of our national pastime. It is true that umpires sometimes make bad calls. Events on the ball field happen fast and umpires' decisions have to be made on the spot without the benefit of thinking it over, talking it over, or instant replay. But far more often than an obviously bad call, players blame the umpire because it's easier than blaming themselves for their own failures. Called third strikes and close calls for a runner on base are the main reasons for blaming the umpire—although there's no excuse for not swinging at a close pitch when there are already two strikes or for not sliding when the throw's on the way.

From the dugout

The umpire's calls are like all of life's tough breaks, unfortunate accidents, and bad coincidences. These are things you have to live with and get over, because they don't change even if they're unfair or wrong. Umpires are human and they make human mistakes. More often, though, their calls are close enough to be right. To blame too much on the umpire ignores the obvious—if the play wasn't that close, it wouldn't have been up to the umpire. When the calls go against you in life, it is sometimes because you weren't a little more careful, a little more skillful. But, other times, the call just goes against you and there's nothing more you could have done to prevent it.

Blame the ump. Blame your teacher. Blame the weather. Blame the other guy. Blame the circumstances. Blame bad luck. But recognize that it may actually be your fault and, even if not, blaming never fixes anything. The umpire never changes his call. Move on.

More from the dugout

Rules are rules, and it's the umpire's job to enforce them. On the baseball field, at home, in school, and in the community, there are people whose job it is to enforce the rules. As unfair as it may feel at times, you have to respect their authority. Respect doesn't mean you can't respectfully discuss and even respectfully disagree. But, the umpires—your parents, teachers, the principal, your boss, the police—will almost always win. And, in most situations, that's what should happen. Rules are for the good of everyone playing the game, including you.

CHAPTER 84

CALLING TIME OUT

The umpire's permission has to be requested to stop the game for any reason. Before the hitter steps out of the batter's box, or the coach walks to the mound, or the runner stands up from his slide to brush himself off and put his hat back on, or the catcher confers with the pitcher, or the pinch runner enters the game, or even before the injured player can be attended to, time out must be called. It's a very simple courtesy to follow, and the umpire almost always gives time out when it's requested; but failing to ask for it makes you look bad and may cause an out for your team.

From the dugout

Courtesy and good manners are important in everything you do. Raising your hand to speak in class, saying "please" and "thank you", letting others speak without interrupting, asking permission to leave the room, clearing your dishes from the dinner table, hanging up your coat, turning off the lights when you leave a room, offering to help around the house, holding the door open for someone behind you, or giving up your seat for someone older. These are simple courtesies to follow; but when you don't, it makes you look bad and makes others think you're inconsiderate or selfish.

CHAPTER 85

THE COACH'S ADVICE

Coaches are just people, and their styles and approaches to coaching are as varied as their personalities. Some coaches are scary and mean; others kindly and grandfatherly. Some think they bring out the best in their players with praise, while others scold; a few may even be abusive. In most situations, their advice is helpful because they have been around and know a lot about the game. It's the coach's job to offer constructive criticism, guiding players to improve their game. Sometimes, though, their advice is not very constructive or useful. It doesn't help a struggling pitcher who can't find the strike zone for the coach to yell, "Just throw strikes". It's not as if the poor pitcher on the mound is *trying* to walk batters and only needs a friendly reminder that strikes are better. A batter stepping into the batter's box in the middle of a long hitting slump doesn't miraculously hit better when his coach screams, "I need you now, we just need a little hit." Hollow advice can have negative effects. The harder a pitcher tries the throw strikes, the less likely he'll succeed. He starts aiming and the ball starts bouncing to the plate or flying over the catcher's head. The more a batter presses to get a hit, the more likely he'll swing at bad pitches and continue to slump.

From the dugout

Be open to constructive criticism from those who have been around and know a lot. Don't feel insulted or threatened by being told how you can improve—use the advice as an opportunity to grow, and as a challenge to become the best you can be. If the way that the advice is given is harsh or less sensitive than you would like, try to hear what they have to say, not how they say it. What's important is the message, not how the messenger says it.

More from the dugout

Telling you the obvious when you're struggling makes you feel even more hopeless and helpless, but it happens a lot. Your coaches, teachers, and even your parents may not realize that you need help identifying *what* you're doing wrong and understanding *how* to fix it, rather than just being reminded that you're not doing a good job. "Make sure you follow through after you release the ball", or "Throw it over the top, not from the side" or "Level out your swing" are useful and helpful suggestions for improvement. When your helpers aren't helping, and their advice sounds hollow, it's ok to ask them—politely and respectfully—for real help. "What am I doing wrong, coach?" "What am I missing on this math problem, Ms. Jones?" "Mom, teach me again how to fold the laundry." Don't be too proud, embarrassed, or stubborn to help your coaches in life to better help you. They will appreciate that you are willing and eager to learn, and that you value their opinion on how to do better.

CHAPTER 86

THE COACH'S SIGNS

As the batter steps to the plate, or the runner on base starts his leadoff, attention turns to the 3rd base coach. The coach goes through a spasm of hand signs and body touches that secretly code for instructions to his batter and runner. Hidden among what seem like random movements are the coach's plans for his players—bunt, steal, "take" (don't swing), hit and run. The coach is in charge, the leader and brains of the team, directing the game from his "box" near third base. Pity the player who misses a sign and doesn't bunt on cue, doesn't steal when told to, or swings at a pitch he was supposed to "take".

From the dugout

It's important to see the signs and to follow the instructions. Independence is nice, but not when the outcome of the game depends on teamwork and strategy. Even if you don't agree with the leader's instructions during a team or group activity, you need to follow them. The person put in charge is in that position because their experience and wisdom is greater than yours. If it turns out badly because of, or despite, you doing what you're told, it's the coach's "fault", not yours. If, on the other hand, you *don't* follow the instructions and there's a bad outcome, expect to be benched.

More from the dugout

There are rare, but important times when you have to disobey the coach or another person in charge. If someone tells you to do something that you know is wrong, because it's dangerous, against the law, or different from what you've been taught is okay to do, you have to refuse and report that person to your parents or to another adult that you trust. Unfortunately, coaches, teachers, scout leaders, and other people you depend on occasionally abuse their position. Your own sense of what's right and what's wrong has to take over if that happens, and you need to get help right away, without feeling guilty or embarrassed.

CHAPTER 87

THANKS, COACH

At the end of the game, as teams are packing up and cleaning up, a few players remember to thank their coach. Very few. Some coaches are paid, most volunteer their time. All appreciate being appreciated. Most even say, "thank you" back. And they smile when you've thanked them.

From the dugout

On the baseball field, at school, at home, and anywhere else that people spend time and effort trying to help you, they deserve your thanks. Your parents drive you to your games and everywhere else, make your lunch, kiss your scrapes and bruises until they feel better, love you for who you are, and prepare you for life. Your brothers and sisters share their experiences and offer their advice, even if you don't ask for it. Your teachers plan each lesson, grade each assignment, worry about what you've learned. Your doctor fixes what hurts, even if the cure sometimes hurts as much. The bus driver greets you in the morning and afternoon, and gets you to school and back safely. Your friends support you on your down days and make your up days more fun. Let those who help you know that you appreciate them. Saying "thanks" is easy. A one word speech, with no rehearsal needed. Takes just a second, but watch the smile that it brings.

CHAPTER 88

AVERAGES

Of all the numbers and statistics in baseball, the most important are season averages. A batting average of 0.300 or more is excellent—that translates into 3 hits for every 10 at bats. A pitcher's earned run average of 2.00 or less is also excellent—2 runs or less allowed in a full game.

From the dugout

Excellent is very different than perfect. If your batting average is 0.300, it means that you *didn't* get a hit 7 times out of 10. If your earned run average is 2.00, it means you *couldn't* prevent 2 earned runs each game. But both averages mean you've done a great job. Failures are part of life. When you focus on any one failure, you're forgetting that the next time you try you'll have another chance to improve your average. And it's the average that counts most, because it measures how well you've done, and how consistent and reliable you have been, over the whole season. Any one bad outcome is a learning opportunity, a chance to be smarter and do better on your next at-bat or the next time you're on the mound. While it's great to aim for perfection, never be disappointed with "just" being excellent.

CHAPTER 89

PRACTICE

Ask any player or coach—games are more fun than practice; that's why they're called games. But, all aspects of baseball, each skill and every performance, are improved by practice. Muscle memory is created with each practice swing of the bat, throw of the ball, and slide into base. Practice strengthens existing talent, teaches new knowledge, and develops new skills. Players who don't practice don't make the team. Teams that don't practice don't win.

From the dugout

School is practice for life. Homework is practice. Studying for tests is practice. Classroom lessons are practice. The more you practice your school skills, the more you learn, the better your test scores, the stronger your grades, and the greater your achievements in life. The muscle memory you get from homework, studying, and classroom learning is your knowledge base for the rest of your life. Practice can be tough—on the baseball field and in school. The workout is hard, the hour may be late, and your energy and enthusiasm can run low. But when you take the field for your next game, every minute of practice pays off. Without practice, your play is rusty and your confidence is shaken. Without practice, your chances of winning are bad, and you may not even make the team.

 CHAPTER 90

WARMING UP

Warm-up is the pre-game ritual that jolts a player's "muscle memory" back to life. Right before a game, players "loosen their arms", "get their gloves working", and "groove their swing". Regardless of how many hours of practice that week on *non-game* days, warm-ups on *game days* are essential. Otherwise the wild throws, bobbled grounders, and awkward strikeouts remind the players that the opposite of warm is cold.

From the dugout

No matter how many times you've done something, and even if you just practiced yesterday, you start out cold each day. Give yourself "warm-up" time before all important tasks, tests, presentations, and performances. Warm-up should be as close to "game time" as possible so that there's less time for you to get distracted from your focus after you've warmed up. Wake up an hour earlier on big test days to go over the material one more time. Get to the auditorium early for your concert and play your piece, or sing your scales, right before the audience gets there. Review your notes right before your big speech to remember the points you want to stress. With your last minute review and preparation right before game time, you refocus yourself, the haze and daze in your head clear, and your brain's "muscle memory" wakes up.

CHAPTER 91

HANDSHAKES

At the end of every game, the winners and losers shake hands. Each team lines up and walks past each other in a parade until every player on one team has said "good game" to every player on the other team, and sealed it with a "high five" or hand slap. The handshakes end the game in a respectful and sportsmanlike way, and set the stage for a friendly rematch when the teams meet again.

From the dugout

No matter how thrilling the win or how tough the loss, opposing teams, competitors, and rivals should end the game by congratulating each other. Throughout your life, there will be rematches. Those you lost to will be back, as will those you beat. If you *burn* bridges by gloating or moping, it will make facing them next time even harder. On the other hand, by *building* bridges with those you've played against, win or lose, you raise the level of your next meeting with them. You may even find yourselves on the *same* team *off* the field, because opponents who show each other respect may become good friends.

CHAPTER 92

DRAGGING THE FIELD, CLEANING THE DUGOUT

At the end of each game, the field shows the strain. Cleat marks, ruts and ridges, canyons around home plate and on the pitcher's mound are never left for the next game—it is the responsibility of the home team to put the field back into playing shape right after the game. Even if it's a week until the next game and a tornado is in the forecast. Same with the dugout disaster. Overflowing with candy wrappers, empty energy drink bottles, and used band-aids, to say nothing of the actual baseball equipment, dugouts are cleaned corner to corner before going home. An un-groomed field and dirty dugout make the team and its players look bad.

From the dugout

Don't leave today's mess for someone else to clean up tomorrow—it's insulting to whoever arrives next to realize that you assumed they would do your housekeeping for you. Don't even leave a mess for *you* to clean up tomorrow. And, messes aren't just dishes in the sink, dirty laundry on the floor, or junk in the car. They include any troubles or problems that you may be tempted to put off for another day. You'll sleep better if you've taken care of most of today's mess today; tomorrow will come with its own new mess.

More from the dugout

Pay particular attention to your personal dugouts—your play-room, bedroom, dorm room. Although no one else may have to share this mess with you, others see it and it makes you look bad. Your space is a part of you, an outer sign of who you are inside—like the clothes you wear and how you brush your hair. Take pride in showing the best dugout for your team and the other teams to see.

CHAPTER 93

INJURIES

There is plenty of crying in baseball. Injuries are common. They are caused by the ball, the bases, the ground, the bat, the cleats, and by the other players. Baseball injuries can be serious, and even permanent; but most, thankfully, are mild and temporary. After a minor injury, how the play turned out may affect how long a player stays down, how much he cries, and how dramatic he acts. Scraped arms, turned ankles, and bruised shins are magically cured by making the great catch or getting the right call from the umpire. But if the ball drops out of the glove or the umpire doesn't see it the same way as the player, drama follows. A sympathetic crowd of coaches, parents and players gathers around the crying, writhing wounded. The more drama, the greater the sympathy and, the player secretly hopes, the quicker the bad outcome of the play is forgotten.

From the dugout

Along with the many joys of life come the unavoidable disappointments. How you handle the low points is up to you. You can writhe on the ground, hoping that the sympathy of those around you will hide your failures, or you can bounce up and move on to the next play. When you writhe, you are telling the world that you hurt and need sympathy. When you bounce up and "shake off" the hurt, you are saying that even though you hurt, you are ready to move on. Sympathy is replaced by respect for your strength and courage.

More from the dugout

Injuries may take you out of the game, hopefully for just an inning or two. While you're healing, think about others whose problems are not temporary. Friends, classmates, neighbors with disabilities and special needs may never get in the game. Use your temporary pain or weakness to understand the difficulties and challenges facing those who are always left sitting on the sidelines.

CHAPTER 94

SUPERSTITIONS

Baseball players are a superstitious bunch. They wear lucky underwear, don't wash their lucky socks, throw a lucky number of practice pitches, swing a lucky number of practice swings, count the sweat lines on their lucky hats, never step on the unlucky chalk lines, and perform lucky rituals when getting set in the batter's box or on the pitcher's mound. Superstitious players believe that by following their lucky habits and holding onto their lucky charms, good fortune will find their dugout.

From the dugout

Belief is a powerful partner in everything you do. It brings you confidence and strength. If you strongly believe that what you are doing is right and good, you will do it better. If you have doubts about your abilities or about the value of what you're doing, you will fail more often than you succeed. Stepping on the chalk line won't bring you bad luck—unless you believe that it will. If you believe that by accidentally wearing the wrong socks you will play poorly, your confidence will be shaken and your game will be affected. You have some control over every "lucky" or "unlucky" outcome. You can improve your luck by believing in yourself and in what you're doing.

CHAPTER 95

SPITTING

There is nothing about the nature of baseball that can possibly explain why players spend so much time spitting. Players spit before they hit and before they pitch. After they hit, and after they pitch. When playing infield and when playing outfield. In the dugout, in the on deck circle, in the bullpen. How did this habit develop? In the old days, baseball players became spitters because of all the time they spent sitting around the dugout chewing tobacco. Today, players spit to imitate cool teammates or famous players they see and want to be like.

From the dugout

Spitting is strong proof of the power of role models. Players who have never tried chewing tobacco spit sunflower seeds. Players who don't spit seeds spit saliva. They stuff as many pieces of chewing gum as they can fit in their cheeks to look like tobacco chewers. Unfortunately, there are many more habits and behaviors of "role models" that are equally disgusting—and more dangerous—than spitting. Pick your role models carefully. The best athletes may be who you want to become on the ball field, but they may not be who you want to be off the field. The older kids at school may seem cool, but some of their habits and behaviors may be better to avoid than to imitate. Find the good qualities that you admire and respect in people, and model yourself after those qualities, but not necessarily after the people themselves—especially if they spit! Your best role model may turn out to be a combination of the best features of many important people in your life.

More from the dugout

Remember that others may be looking to *you* for inspiration and role modeling. Be aware that how you behave, what you say, and what you do may influence those around you who look up to you. This is especially true of younger brothers and sisters who have close-up views of you and what you do. Act in ways that you would want those who are watching you, learning from you, and admiring you, to act.

CHAPTER 96

BIOLOGY

Nowhere are the amazing differences in biology more obvious than on a baseball field. Players of the same age can be very, very different in size, speed, and strength. Those differences can change how the game turns out; and, they are what everybody is talking about in the bleachers. The biggest, fastest, and strongest usually hit the ball farther, steal more bases, and pitch the ball harder than the smaller and slower players. But, while baseball biology can be unfair and even cruel, it can also be *overcome* by skills that have nothing to do with physical gifts—attitude, hustle, hard work, and mastering the fundamentals of hitting, fielding, and pitching.

From the dugout

Everyone is born with a different "package". Some packages are big, fast, and strong, others aren't. Some are physically beautiful, others mentally sharper. Those who succeed in baseball and in life combine their "package" with new skills they gain by living every day. Enthusiasm, extra effort, commitment, motivation, and self-discipline are skills that you can choose to develop, or not. So are generosity, thoughtfulness, kindness, and a winning personality. The package you're born with is neither a guarantee of success nor an excuse for failure—it only determines where your home plate is, where you start. How far you get around life's base path will be determined by you and by how successful you are at making the most of your package.

More from the dugout

Look beyond the physical package to find a person's potential contributions. Your shortest friends may be the fastest runners or the infielders with the best hands; or maybe they just are able to get on base more often because they are "small strike zones". The least coordinated player on your team may be the most valuable teammate in the dugout because of his attitude and his sportsmanship. Your disabled classmate may be a great 1st base coach or team manager or official scorekeeper. Success in life, like success on the field, requires a long list of contributions from people with different skills, abilities, and packages. The most important features of a person come from inside, and to see them and appreciate them, you can't be blinded by anyone's outer package.

CHAPTER 97

RALLIES

As depressing as trailing in a big game can be, rallying from behind to take over the lead is one of most thrilling experiences a team can have. Players will remember a come-from-behind win much longer than winning a game they were leading all along. Each rally is triggered by a first breakthrough—a timely hit, a patient walk, a daring stolen base. That lead step is followed by others, each building on the one before as the goal gets closer, until at last the winning run scores.

From the dugout

As teammates pile on the hero who had the last hit, walk, or steal to win the game, the real hero is the first player who began the rally. Leadership means stepping up when your team needs you. When the odds are against you, your back is to the wall, and failure is likely, even expected. Leadership means ignoring the odds and the expectations. It means never quitting, even when it seems like losing is a sure thing. A leader taps his inner strength, overcomes his inner fears, acts on his strong beliefs, and finds a way to get on base so that others have the chance to follow. A leader knows that big things start with little things and that you lead by setting an example. And, a leader doesn't need his team to pile their gratitude on him; he's comfortable with the glory going to his teammates, who wisely followed his lead.

CHAPTER 98

CLUTCH AND CLENCH

Clutch is performance under pressure. The clutch hitter comes through with the base hit when the game's on the line and there are runners on base. The clutch pitcher throws strikes, and strikeouts, with bases loaded and the other team's best hitter at the plate. Clench is the opposite of clutch; it's what happens to a player who tightens up during tough situations and cannot perform, cannot produce.

From the dugout

The difference between clutch and clench is a matter of control. Do you control the situation or does the situation control you? A clutch performer is able to separate himself from the circumstances, ignoring the base runners, the game score, the screaming fans. He trusts in himself and his abilities, not rattled by the roar around him. But, a player who clenches lets the events overwhelm him, overpowering his talent, experience, and confidence. Will you be clutch, or will you clench? The answer may depend on whether you just *step* to the plate or *strut* to the plate, on whether you *drag yourself* to the mound or *swagger* to the mound. When you enter a tense situation in your life, strut and swagger. It doesn't have to be obvious on the outside, but you have to feel strut and swagger inside. You are the cream of the crop, the best of the bunch, the master of the moment. You are smarter and know more about the subject than anyone else in the room. Your fingers own the piano, your singing is the sweetest at the tryouts, your fastball is un-hittable. Control the room, command the game, convince the crowd. Be clutch.

More from the dugout

The need to perform under pressure is part of everyone's life at some time and, for certain people, it is a regular occurrence. Some people love high-tension situations where they feel they alone can win because they are so clutch. Team captain, group leader, student council president, graduation speaker, orchestra soloist, program director, crew chief, shift supervisor. Others clench at tense moments and dread high-pressure situations, making their life decisions based on avoiding stress at any cost. Most people are somewhere in between—preferring not to be under pressure very often, but usually able to be clutch when needed; if they can just strut and swagger their way through today's high stress, things will be easier tomorrow. Know yourself. Hard work is a requirement for success, but constant stress is not. If you are more happy being on the team, but not leading it, that's important to discover about yourself. If you are not the kind of person who loves and lives for chaos, crisis, and clutch moments, find paths in your life that don't demand such high intensity.

CHAPTER 99

STREAKS AND SLUMPS

The momentum of baseball affects individual players and whole teams. Players may go many games without a hit and then suddenly break through and start a red-hot batting streak. Teams may win 5 games in a row only to lose the next 6. Each hit or win builds on itself, as does each strikeout and loss. Momentum takes on a life of its own. Teams with a "winning mentality" keep winning—until they lose. Then their confidence is shaken, their mentality now a losing one. A hitter who keeps failing thinks of himself as a failure until he gets a hit or two—and then his confidence returns, his self-image improves. But, at the end of the season, the player and team with the most *balanced* performances will be the most successful. Winning more than losing, hitting more than striking out—but neither extreme in the extreme.

From the dugout

The worse a slump is, the better the streak that follows it feels. And, as thrilling as a streak may be, the next slump brings the high to a crashing low. Cycling between high peaks and low valleys in your life can be upsetting and unhealthy. Find balance. You have to learn to interrupt the cycles, break the momentum—of both the very high highs and the very low lows. Your "mentality" should be a realistic, balanced, and steady one; no one is *always* a winner or *always* a loser. Know that some days will be better than others, some experiences happier and some sadder. But don't let your momentum carry you too high or too low. Even though you try to win most of the time, there will be losses. And losses don't make you a loser.

CHAPTER 100

A GAME OF INCHES

A pitch just slightly higher, a swing just slightly lower, a bounce just slightly cleaner, a dive just slightly farther, a throw just slightly closer. Games are won and lost by tiny margins, millimeters of airspace that separate the champions from the runners-up. The winners almost never remember that they came so very close to losing; but the losers linger on what might have been had they been just inches closer.

From the dugout

Many accomplishments in your life are determined by the tiniest of margins. Be humble. Remember that without the right bounce, the right combination of luck and timing, someone other than you might have won. You should be proud of your achievement and the praise that comes with it, but never so proud that you forget how close winning is to losing. It's a game of inches. The humility you show in your success today will help you handle a failure tomorrow. But gloating and boasting today will make future disappointments all the more embarrassing.

More from the dugout

Failures are also often by just inches. When you fail, don't lose perspective—and put losing in perspective. There may be very little separating you from the winners. Falling short this time doesn't predict how you will do in the future; it should encourage you to try even harder the next time. When an inch here or there can make the difference between being a champion or the runner-up, do everything in you power to get the extra inch. But not every inch is in your power. All you can do is try to control the things you have control over, and keep trying until the ball bounces a few inches closer.

CHAPTER 101

HEROES AND GOATS

Most teams have a couple of stars—players who consistently hit the farthest, pitch the fastest, field the smoothest. But the stars are not always the heroes. In fact, most baseball games are not won by the stars, because there are fewer stars than there are just regular players. In any one game, any regular player can become a hero for that game. Players may become heroes by hitting home runs or pitching shutout innings, but often it's with less dramatic acts. They may walk or get hit by a pitch and force in their team's winning run. They may drive in the winning run with a bloop single or a ground-ball that's misplayed. They may come in from the bullpen just to get the other team's last batter to ground out. They may steal home on a pitcher's wild pitch. The hero's teammates pile on him and he goes home with a giant smile, a hero for the day. But for every hero, there's also a goat: the pitcher who gave up the home run, walk, wild pitch, or bloop single; the fielder who misplayed the ball; the hitter who struck out with bases loaded. The goat's teammates turn their eyes away and he goes home in tears.

From the dugout

Today's hero is tomorrow's goat, and today's goat may be tomorrow's hero. Every game offers new chances for success and for failure. Unless you're that rare superstar whose heroic accomplishments are so much more common than failures, your hero or goat role today is likely to change by tomorrow. Celebrate today's success, but remember that it may have happened because of someone else's failure. Be prepared for tomorrow's disappointments when someone else may succeed at your expense. And when that happens, remember that if you keep playing, soon it will be your turn to be the hero again.

More from the dugout

It can be tough being one of the stars on the team, because stars are expected to be heroes all the time. When stars become goats, as the law of averages requires from time to time, the failed expectations can be overwhelming. Just because you're talented and usually succeed, don't set the bar too high. Think like the star player you are, but cut yourself some slack. Even stars fail, but true stars rise again.

978-0-595-42390-3
0-595-42390-6